THE HERESY OF THE SINNER'S PRAYER

Or

The Deception and Damnation of the Sinner's Prayer

Written by
Robert Breaker III

5th Edition

Copyright 2006

ISBN-13: 978-1463756390

ISBN-10: 1463756399

𝔅reaker's

AV
1611

𝔓ublications

> "*Many people believe that a sinner cannot be saved without a period of prayer, without consciously calling upon God. However, the Bible does not say that a sinner must pray in order to be saved. In fact, immediately following the verse in Rom. 10:13 is an explanation which shows that calling on God is an evidence of faith in the heart and that it is really faith which settles the matter... No matter how long he prays, if he does not trust in Christ, he can never be saved. If he trusts in Christ without conscious prayer, then he is saved already. There is just one plan of salvation and just one step a sinner must take to secure it. That step is to believe on the Lord Jesus Christ!*"
>
> **- Dr. John R. Rice**

All scripture given in this booklet is from the King James Authorized 1611 English Bible.

Introduction

For well over one hundred years now, many denominations, Soul Winners, Pastors, Missionaries, and even Evangelists have been telling people that all they have to do to be saved is simply recite *The Sinner's Prayer.* So strong is this modernistic teaching that most of Christianity today believes that a person can *only* be saved by *repeating the Sinner's Prayer.* But is this Biblical? Did Christ or the Apostles teach that salvation is simply obtained by *repeating a formal prayer* pronounced from one's mouth? Does a person really get to heaven by the proverbial *wing and A PRAYER?*

The answer, my friend, most certainly is, "No!" The cold, hard fact is that the Bible teaches salvation is not by prayer at all, rather by GRACE through FAITH (Eph. 2:8,9) in the SHED BLOOD of the Lord Jesus Christ (Rom. 3:25) plus nothing, minus nothing!

This might sound foreign to some people, especially those who adhere to the Sinner's Prayer mentality as the plan of salvation. However the Bible is clear when it teaches us that salvation comes by *faith* from the *HEART*, not by *a repetitious prayer* spoken only from *THE MOUTH.*

So where does this *Sinner's Prayer* concept come from? Who invented the idea that a person can obtain heaven by something they *say* or *repeat?* And why are so many nowadays preaching this instead of the true Gospel of GRACE through FAITH in JESUS and his bloody sacrifice for the forgiveness of sin? These questions and more will be dealt with in this booklet.

The Bible clearly teaches us we are now in the Laodicean Church Age, a time of great apostasy, in which the Church as a whole has kicked God out the door (Rev. 3:20). It is running things *its* way instead of *God's* way. Because of this, many false doctrines have arisen within the Church, which are completely foreign to the Bible. These are *man's teachings* instead of *God's commandments*. Telling a person that his *PRAYER* will save him is one of these doctrines.

In these last days, apostate Bible Teachers, Preachers, and Soul winners, have either willingly or unwittingly turned from the Biblical means of salvation by solely *trusting in what Christ has DONE for you*, into a vain religious ritual of *pressuring a man to DO something to be saved.* Usually this ritual consists of a instructing a person to "Pray" or "Repeat" the Sinner's Prayer." And then that person is assured he is saved because of his verbal incantation.

When a person doubts, which people like this always do, the remedy he is given by other Christians is to simply pray the Sinner's Prayer all over again for "assurance."

This usually leaves the Sinner believing that the *prayer itself* is the *saving medium*, and not Jesus Christ alone, and because of this the Sinner is left religious, but lost. He has been deceived into trusting his *SPEAKING* rather than instructed from the Bible to rest solely upon the atoning *SACRIFICE* of Christ by faith.

True Christians should then be faithful in exposing this modern apostate teaching and pointing Sinners only to Christ crucified, and salvation through Him alone by faith in his finished blood atonement. Salvation is all about what *Jesus has done*, not what *we have done or can do*.

Dear reader, I challenge you to read this booklet through and make sure of your salvation by *examining yourself* (2 Cor. 13:5). What are you trusting in to get you to heaven? If it's Jesus and his shed blood alone, then you are saved and on your way to heaven! But, if you are trusting in your Sinner's Prayer, that *you did*, instead of *resting completely* upon the finished work of Jesus Christ, then you are lost! What are you trusting in to save you—a prayer you *SAID* or the blood God *SHED*?

Preface

Several years ago, a Preacher told the following story of shallow soul winning. I paraphrase:

*"I visited a Roman Catholic family and witnessed to them for about half an hour. At the close of my presentation, I asked them if they would like to receive Jesus Christ as their Saviour and be saved. They quickly responded, 'No thank you!' So I asked them if I could have a word of prayer before I left and they allowed me to do so. But I noticed that when I prayed, they repeated all my words. I then thought I'd lead them in **the Sinner's Prayer**, and I did. They followed each of my words entirely, and then I left. Afterwards, I told my visitation partner, 'I LED THOSE PEOPLE TO THE LORD AND THEY DIDN'T EVEN KNOW IT!'"*

Now, the person who told this story later denied saying something so foolish, and claimed it never happened. But, I've since heard similar stories just like this one, where some prideful Soul Winner uses the same words: *"I LED A GUY TO THE LORD AND HE DIDN'T EVEN KNOW IT!"*

But, can a person get saved without *"knowing it?"* Is it possible for someone to be saved against his will? Can tricking a person into repeating the Sinner's Prayer really grant him eternal life?

The Biblical answer is a dogmatic, "NO!" Salvation is not a matter of the *LIPS*, rather a matter of the *HEART*.

For a sinner to get saved, several things must happen. First, he must *hear* the Gospel with his *ears*, and then he must *understand* with his *heart* before he can be converted. The words of Jesus in Matthew 13:14-15, show us clearly that *hearing* and *understanding* are essential to salvation:

"14 **And in them is fulfilled the prophecy of Esaias, which saith, By hearing ye shall hear, and shall not understand; and seeing ye shall see, and shall not perceive:** 15 **For this**

people's heart is waxed gross, and their ears are dull of hearing, and their eyes they have closed; lest at any time they should see with their eyes and HEAR WITH THEIR EARS, AND SHOULD UNDERSTAND WITH THEIR HEART, and SHOULD BE CONVERTED..."

Understanding must come from the HEART. And for a Sinner to be saved, it is a matter of the *heart*, not just the *mouth*. A lost person must *want* to be saved of his own accord after he hears and understands the Gospel. He must come to God himself, and not be coaxed into it by others.

Thus, it's IMPOSSIBLE for a person to get saved and *"NOT EVEN KNOW IT!"*

Modern Christianity as a whole, however, doesn't understand this simple Biblical truth. It has departed from the Biblical means of salvation by GRACE THROUGH FAITH, and is guilty of preaching the heresy *that salvation is not by heartfelt faith in Christ at all*, but rather *one's repeating a prayer to Christ*. In other words, they claim that God's saving power is not through FAITH ALONE in Christ's ATONING SACRIFICE, but rather by man's own ACTION of SPEAKING the Sinner's Prayer.

So ingrained is this heretical teaching among so-called Fundamentalists and Evangelicals, that they have developed a "1-2-3 REPEAT AFTER ME" method of soul winning which omits the Gospel in it's entirety and *tricks* a Sinner into praying a VAIN RELIGIOUS PRAYER, begging God for forgiveness. But does a man get saved *by* his prayer? Will God forgive anyone who comes to Him *seeking* salvation from the mouth apart from *trusting* the BLOODSTAINED GOSPEL OF CHRIST from the heart? Most certainly not!

The Scriptures are clear, no one gets saved by a vain, religious prayer, and no one can be *tricked* into getting saved against their will. To be saved, a sinner must REPENT (Mk. 1:15; Luke 13:3). Repentance comes from the *heart*, not the *mouth*! A sinner must come to the realization that Jesus died

4

for his sins in his place. He must then believe upon the Lord Jesus Christ (John 6:47), receiving his finished work on Calvary by faith as sufficient to give him the new birth. Repentance is the key to salvation. For anyone can easily *repeat a prayer*. But without *repentance,* the prayer is useless.

Jesus speaks of those who think that salvation is just a matter of the MOUTH and not the *heart* in the following negative way: "...**Well hath Esaias prophesied of you hypocrites, as it is written, This people honoureth me WITH THEIR LIPS, but THEIR HEART IS FAR FROM ME. Howbeit in vain do they worship me, teaching for doctrines the commandments of men.**" (Mark 7:6,7)

Here, Jesus speaks to the Pharisees, or the lost religious crowd, who instead of teaching God's doctrine, taught the commandments of man. They spoke of God with the *lips*, but their *heart* was far from him.

The same has happened with modern Christianity today. As it apostatizes and becomes more Phariseeical, it too puts more emphasis on the MOUTH instead of the HEART.

So dogmatical is its stance against sound Biblical doctrine, many popular Fundamentalist preachers have even begun calling *REPENTANCE* an "*enemy of the Gospel.*" (Can you imagine such a thing?)

With this in mind, the author saw the need to write a book such as this one, exposing the "*heresy*" of the Sinner's Prayer—that is to say, the "*heresy*" of deceiving a lost person into believing that if he will just repeat some mystical incantation he'll go to heaven.

The truth of the matter is NO MATTER HOW MANY PRAYERS A PERSON PRAYS, HE'LL NEVER GET SAVED UNTIL HE FIRST REALIZES HE IS A SINNER, HEARS THE GOSPEL, and PUTS HIS COMPLETE FAITH AND TRUST IN THE SHED BLOOD OF THE DYING LAMB OF GOD!"

Now before going any farther let me dogmatically state the sound doctrinal truth that *a person can be saved WHEN he prays,* but *a person is not saved BY his prayer.* The problem with those who teach the Sinner's prayer is that they usually don't state this simply fact. Instead of pointing people to Christ alone as the *SAVING PROPITIATION,* many a modern Soul Winner usually gives a *SHALLOW PRESENTATION* of the Gospel (or omits it in its entirety), and then tells a person that if he'll just *repeat* the Sinner's Prayer then God will save him. This has deceived countless millions of people into thinking *the actual prayer itself is what saves them,* instead of simple *faith in God's substitutionary blood atonement.*

I've personally met many people whose testimony of salvation is, *"Well, I repeated the prayer!"* But where is their faith in Jesus' blood?

When the lives of such people are examined, they usually have no fruit of salvation, no desire to serve the Lord, and absolutely no spiritual growth. In fact, many people like this live more worldly than most unsaved people! Why is this? Could it be the person has missed salvation and is still left lost?

This can be the only explanation if the Sinner is trusting in the *prayer he prayed* to get him to Heaven. He is not saved. He cannot be, for he is guilty of trusting in something he's done in and of himself, rather than trusting only in what Jesus has done for him.

The well-known evangelist Dr. John R. Rice spoke out against the heresy of teaching that prayer saves in the following words:

"Many people believe that a sinner cannot be saved without a period of prayer, without consciously calling upon God. However, the Bible does not say that a sinner must pray in order to be saved. In fact, immediately following the verse in Rom. 10:13 is an explanation which shows that calling on God is an evidence of faith in the heart and that it is really

faith which settles the matter... No matter how long he prays, if he does not trust in Christ, he can never be saved. If he trusts in Christ without conscious prayer, then he is saved already. There is just one plan of salvation and just one step a sinner must take to secure it. That step is to believe on the Lord Jesus Christ!"

Whether a person prays or not, he is saved by FAITH alone. A person can pray and be saved if he BELIEVES while praying. Or a man can believe and be saved without praying at all. THE PRAYER ISN'T THE SAVING MEDIUM, salvation depends upon whether or not a person **REPENTS** and **PUTS HIS COMPLETE TRUST IN THE LORD JESUS CHRIST!**

With this in mind, let us now begin our study on the "Heresy" of the Sinner's Prayer, and see why it's so important to give a clear presentation of the Gospel. For tricking a person into repeating a prayer before he is ready, is to give him a false hope of heaven and a false plan of salvation, which could end up damning him to Hell!

The emphasis should never be on what man CAN DO, but in trusting *wholly* and *completely* upon what JESUS CHRIST DID FOR MAN! It's *HERESY* to say *a prayer saves*, when the Bible clearly teaches JESUS SAVES!

THE SINNER'S PRAYER vs.
THE SAVIOUR'S PROPITIATION

What if you died today and stood *eyeball to eyeball* with Jesus Christ, and He said to you, *"Why I should let you into heaven?"*

Have you ever given any thought to how you would respond to such a question? I'm sure most would say, *"Oh, well I'm a good person, and I've never killed anyone!"*

Others might respond, *"Well, I've tried to live a good life, so I deserve to enter!"*

Another would state, *"I did the best I could to keep your commandments!"*

Yet another might retort, *"I go to church, and I've been baptized, so I did my duty."*

All of these answers might sound like good reasons to the typical lost person who thinks salvation is based upon *his own merits*, but not to God! According to the Bible, salvation is not obtained by what a MAN DOES (Titus 3:5), but rather *by faith in what* GOD DID FOR MAN (Gal. 2:16), when He gave himself as the ultimate sacrifice for sinners to pay for the sins of the whole world (Gal. 1:4; 1 John 4:10).

Biblically, salvation is GOD'S FREE GIFT (Rom. 6:23), offered to ALL sinners (1 Tim. 2:4-6). But only those who RECEIVE HIM BY FAITH shall be saved and have a right to enter into the pearly gates (Eph. 2:8,9; John 1:12).

With this in mind, how then would *you*, dear reader, answer the above question? If your answer begins with, *"I..."* then you most likely have shown you believe you deserve heaven based on something *YOU DID*. This is very anti-biblical! And, *you are guilty of the greatest blasphemy the world has ever known!* You are saying that Christ's death on the cross is *meaningless* and entirely *unable to save you.* Y*ou are guilty of trying to take Christ's place*, by *making yourself your own saviour. You are trying to get to heaven by what you do, rather than accepting what Jesus has already done for you. You are trying to obtain heaven by* *your own WORKS, rather than simply accepting the WORK of God at Calvary.* This offends God more than the most heinous sin ever committed by mankind!

Men try to justify themselves before God in many ways. Some think they deserve God's favor because they are *religious*. Others think God owes them the pleasures of heaven because of their *good works*. While many believe that if they are *baptized, confirmed*, or *pray enough* then God will have to accept them for their ritualistic self-sacrifice.

But the truth is all man's righteousnesses are as filthy rags (Isa. 64:6). There is none good, no not one! (Rom. 3:10). All have sinned and come short of the glory of God (Rom. 3:23). Because of this, all a man does, every *thought*, every *action*, every *prayer*, every *word*, and every *desire* is an *abomination* to God, because it is the work of a sinful being that has rejected Him.

In contrast, there is no story so wonderful as the Biblical story of redemption. God himself came down to a sin-stricken world to die for sinful mankind. He that knew no sin, became *sin* (2 Cor. 5:21) and took God's chastisement upon himself (Isa. 53:4,5) in our place for our sins (1 John 3:5)! Oh what boundless love!

He paid a debt He did not owe for people that did not love Him; in a place He didn't want to go, He rose again to bring man unto Him! What a wonderful Saviour is the Lord Jesus Christ!

After claiming victory over death, hell, sin, and the grave, He returned to His rightful throne in Heaven. All He asks now is for man to *repent* (feel sorrow for their sins) and accept Him (by turning from his *own sinful righteousness*, to Christ's *righteousness*—from *his own works* to trusting *God's finished work on Calvary!*)

Sadly, most men of today have done anything but. The history of the Church Age is a battle between true Christians, pointing Sinners to the cross, and false religions pressuring men to perform useless rituals in the hopes of obtaining forgiveness.

God is not pleased with anyone who teaches a man must *DO SOMETHING* to be saved. His plan of salvation is not "say this," "repeat that," "follow this," or "do that." Nay, GOD'S PLAN OF SALVATION IS FOR A PERSON TO COME TO JESUS and RECEIVE HIM BY FAITH, trusting HIS WORK alone on Calvary, with no mixture of his *own goodness*.

No man can save himself. He must have a *Saviour* who can do this for him. That Saviour is the Lord Jesus Christ (Acts 4:12), who SHED HIS BLOOD on the cross as *THE PROPITIATION* for the sins of the world (1 John 4:10).

The Biblical way then to answer Jesus in our aforementioned hypothetical question of why he should let us into heaven, would be two little words: "**THE BLOOD.**"

For it is only through faith in the *shed blood* of Jesus Christ (Rom. 3:25) that a Sinner can be justified before God (Rom. 5:9) and gain access to heaven (Heb. 10:19). The blood of Jesus *cleanses from all sin* (1 John 1:7), *redeems* (Col. 1:14), *forgives* (Eph. 1:7) and *makes peace with God* (Col. 1:20)!

This is why man can't obtain his own salvation apart from Jesus Christ's shed blood on Calvary. He cannot make it to heaven on his own, nor can he sacrifice himself. He must find a substitute—someone who's willing to die in his place. Only Jesus Christ was willing to do this!

However, just because God died for the sins of the world doesn't mean the whole world is going to heaven. Every person in this world must avail themselves of Christ's substitutionary sacrifice by FAITH.

Hebrews 11:6 states, "**But without faith it is impossible to please him; for he that cometh to God must believe that he is, and that he is a rewarder of them that diligently seek him.**"

This verse states dogmatically that it is IMPOSSIBLE to come to God by one's own works! God demands FAITH. And when a person comes to God by faith in the precious shed blood of Jesus (Rom. 3:25), he receives the Holy Spirit and Eternal Life.

Ephesians 1:13 confirms this, by saying, "**In whom ye also trusted, after that ye heard the word of truth, the gospel of your salvation: in whom also after that ye believed, ye were sealed with that holy Spirit of promise.**"

Biblically, a person who trusts Christ's finished work— His shed blood on Calvary—receives eternal life *immediately*, at the very moment he believes. This is salvation. It's by COMPLETE FAITH in CHRIST'S FINISHED WORK!

Compare this now with the modern teaching of the "*Sinner's Prayer*" (an expression that's never found in the Bible). Many modern religious people tell a person that all they have to do to get to heaven is simply, "repeat the Sinner's Prayer." But is this Biblical? Does a person really obtain heaven by DOING this apart from UNDERSTANDING the Gospel, and BELIEVING upon the Lord Jesus Christ?

There are some who adhere to the Sinner's Prayer that would be quick to say, "Yes." However, what saith the Scriptures?

In Romans 10:14-16, we read:

How then shall they call on him in whom they have not believed? and how shall they believe in him of whom they have not heard? and how shall they hear without a preacher? And how shall they preach, except they be sent? as it is written, How beautiful are the feet of them that preach the gospel of peace, and bring glad tidings of good things! But they have not all obeyed the gospel. For Esaias saith, Lord, who hath believed our report?

According to the Bible, a person *must* first hear the Gospel preached, *before* they can *believe* the report. They must learn of Christ's sacrifice on the cross and understand what HE'S DONE FOR THEM. Then, their faith must be in Christ alone!

This is very important, because we have many shallow soul winners running around today claming that if a person will just *repeat* a simple prayer, then he'll go to heaven, whether he *understands* or *has heard* the Gospel or not. They claim God will save him anyway because of his *sincerity*. But this is strictly unbiblical!

If a person *sincerely* repeats a prayer, *trusting he'll be saved because of it*, he has made salvation based upon his ACT of praying, instead of by FAITH alone in the ATONING WORK of Christ.

Herein lies the **heresy** of the "Sinner's Prayer." It turns men from God and what he's done to themselves and what they do.

Allow me to dogmatically state that *I'm not against anyone uttering a prayer*. But I do believe *it is a grievous heresy to tell someone that they can get to heaven BY their PRAYER*. It is true that a person can be saved WHEN he prays, but he doesn't receive eternal life BECAUSE of his prayer. There is a *fine line*, but a *huge difference*.

To tell a person that a *prayer* is all it takes to get to heaven is to give him a false assurance of heaven. For no where in the Bible are we told a person is saved *BY* prayer. Rather we are told that a person is saved by GRACE through FAITH (Eph. 2:8,9) alone.

Thus, if a lost soul is led in a *Sinner's Prayer* without the Holy Spirit showing him his lost condition, nor having heard and understood the Gospel, that sinner will always *trust in his prayer, instead of the blood of Jesus* shed at Calvary, and he will be left eternally lost!

Clearly people like this are trusting in what THEY DID, instead of what Christ Jesus DID FOR THEM. This is the *damnation* of the Sinner's Prayer.

Therefore, it's important every Soul Winner makes sure he tells lost souls about *sin, righteousness,* and *judgment* (John 16:8). For a lost sinner will never get saved until he first sees himself as an *unworthy Sinner (unrighteous)* bound for *God's judgment* (Hell), in need of trusting Christ's *righteousness* instead of his own.

It's sad that modern, apostate Christianity has departed from preaching the Gospel of Christ's blood atonement. Sadder still that they've replaced it with a non-offensive, mechanical, salesman's presentation of showing a Sinner only a few verses and then giving them a quick invitation to "repeat a prayer." This has led countless millions into thinking that salvation is dependent upon the ACTION of SPEAKING, instead of by faith alone in Christ's ATONING SACRIFICE on the cross. This is the great *deception* of the Sinner's Prayer.

The simple fact is no matter how many prayers a person prays, he'll never obtain God's free gift of eternal life until he gives up trusting his own self-righteousness (i.e. his sinner's prayer), and takes Christ's righteousness by FAITH!

Or as the famous Dr. Peter S. Ruckman once so amply put it, "...*Until he* [the Sinner] *sees his own goodness can't save him, the prayers* [he prays] *don't amount to a hill of beans!*"

Because the sanguine, blood-stained Gospel of Jesus Christ has been omitted so much in modern preaching among so-called Christians, let's begin by looking at exactly what the Gospel is. For it is very different from the Sinner's Prayer plan of salvation which claims a person is saved only by what they *say*.

THE GOSPEL ACCORDING TO THE BIBLE

The Bible tells us exactly what the Gospel is in 1 Corinthians fifteen and verses one through four:

1 Moreover, brethren, I declare unto you the gospel which I preached unto you, which also ye have received, and wherein ye stand; 2 By which also ye are saved, if ye keep in memory what I preached unto you, unless ye have believed in vain. 3 For I delivered unto you first of all that which I also received, how that Christ died for our sins according to the scriptures; 4 and that he was buried, and that he rose again the third day according to the scriptures.

The Gospel then is the *death*, *burial*, and *resurrection* of Jesus Christ. It is what *JESUS DID* on the cross of Calvary. And one is saved (vs 2) by *BELIEVING* (or trusting) in what Jesus DID, not what a person DOES in or of himself. This distinction is very important, and Paul even makes it himself in verse two when he mentions that it's possible for one to "**believe in vain.**"

To believe in *vain* means that someone is believing in *themselves*. Those then that believe in vain are those trusting in something *THEY DID*, rather than what Christ Jesus *HAS DONE* for them.

The modern "Sinner's Prayer" teaching often leaves a person trusting in *their prayer* rather than Jesus' *propitiatory* finished work on Calvary.

The Gospel, then, is all about *Jesus* and all about *believing* what he has done in paying for our sins. To come to Jesus in prayer apart from believing the Gospel would then be to come to Jesus another way, and would be expecting God to save you based upon what you do, not based upon what God has done for you.

Thus, telling a person they can be saved by the Sinner's Prayer alone is to deceive a person, and to divert their faith from trusting only in the Gospel. This is a grievous heresy.

SALVATION BY GRACE THROUGH FAITH

According to the Bible, salvation for us today in the Church Age is only by *Faith*. There are countless verses in the New Testament to prove this, such as:

For by grace are ye saved through faith; and that not of yourselves: *it is* **the gift of God: Not of works, lest any man should boast.** (Ephesians 2:8,9)

Therefore we conclude that a man is justified by faith without the deeds of the law. (Rom 3:28)

Wherefore the law was our schoolmaster *to bring us* **unto Christ, that we might be justified by faith.** (Gal 3:24)

For ye are all the children of God by faith in Christ Jesus. (Gal 3:26)

Faith is defined in the Bible as, "...**the substance of things hoped for, the evidence of things not seen**" (Heb. 11:1). In other words, faith is completely trusting in someone or something even though you can't see him or it. Salvation then is by placing your *FAITH* (i.e. believing or trusting) in what Jesus has DONE for you, and not by *DOING* something yourself (such as repeating a prayer or asking or begging God to save you).

THE WORDS OF JESUS

When Jesus preached, he never told anyone to "repeat a prayer to gain eternal life," nor did he instruct them to "ask him to be saved." Jesus always told people that eternal life or salvation was by BELIEVING, as seen in the following verses:

That whosoever believeth in him should not perish, but have eternal life. For God so loved the world, that he gave his only begotten Son, that whosoever believeth in him should not perish, but have everlasting life. (John 3:15,16)

He that believeth on him is not condemned: but he that believeth not is condemned already, because he hath not believed in the name of the only begotten Son of God. (John 3:18)

He that believeth on the Son hath everlasting life: and he that believeth not the Son shall not see life; but the wrath of God abideth on him. (John 3:36)

Verily, verily, I say unto you, He that heareth my word, and believeth on him that sent me, hath everlasting life, and shall not come into condemnation; but is passed from death unto life. (John 5:24)

Jesus answered and said unto them, This is the work of God, that ye believe on him whom he hath sent. (John 6:29)

Verily, verily, I say unto you, He that believeth on me hath everlasting life. (John 6:47)
I said therefore unto you, that ye shall die in your sins: for if ye believe not that I am *he,* ye shall die in your sins. (John 8:24)

Jesus said unto her, I am the resurrection, and the life: he that believeth in me, though he were dead, yet shall he live: And whosoever liveth and believeth in me shall never die. Believest thou this? (John 11:25,26)

THE WORDS OF JOHN

Nor did the apostle John ever tell anyone to pray a "Sinner's Prayer." He too always taught that people are saved only by *believing* (Faith), as seen in the following verses:

The same came for a witness, to bear witness of the Light, that all *men* through him might believe. (John 1:7)

But as many as received him, to them gave he power to become the sons of God, *even* to them that believe on his name. (John 1:12)

But these are written, that ye might believe that Jesus is the Christ, the Son of God; and that believing ye might have life through his name. (John 20:31)

THE WORDS OF PETER

It's the same with the apostle Peter, who taught salvation by *faith*, not by works, nor by *speaking,* as evidenced below:

Then Simon Peter answered him, Lord, to whom shall we go? thou hast the words of eternal life. And we believe and are sure that thou art that Christ, the Son of the living God. (John 6:68,69)

Neither is there salvation in any other: for there is none other name under heaven given among men, whereby we must be saved. (Acts 4:12)

Peter rose up, and said unto them, Men *and* brethren, ye know how that a good while ago God made choice among us, that the Gentiles by my mouth should hear the word of the gospel, and believe. (Acts 15:7)

Wherefore also it is contained in the scripture, Behold, I lay in Sion a chief corner stone, elect, precious: and he that believeth on him shall not be confounded. (1 Pet 2:6)

Peter said only Jesus had the words of eternal life. And he told us salvation comes only through believing in him *after* hearing the Gospel. He never told anyone to "pray" or "beg" God for forgiveness.

In preaching to Cornelius and those with him, we read the following, "**To him give all the prophets witness, that through his name <u>whosoever believeth in him shall receive remission of sins.</u> <u>While Peter yet spake these words, the Holy Ghost fell on all them which heard the word.</u>**" (Acts 10:43,44). These men were saved by FAITH, and they didn't even say a prayer! They simply BELIEVED what Peter preached and were saved because of it!

THE WORDS OF THE APOSTLES THEMSELVES

In Acts chapter fifteen, the Bible says that some men from Judea came to Jerusalem and taught that men had to *do something* to be saved (vs 1). This troubled the early church and the apostles came together to discuss the matter. After seeing Gentiles saved by FAITH (vs 7,8), Peter spoke up concluding with the other apostles:

"But we believe that through the grace of the Lord Jesus Christ we shall be saved, even as they."

Notice what he did *not* say. He did not say, "*We believe that by repeating the Sinner's Prayer, we shall be saved even as they!*" No! Peter, and the early apostles knew that salvation was by God's GRACE through their own FAITH in Him!

THE WORDS OF THE APOSTLE PAUL

Paul is the Apostle to the Gentiles (Romans 11:13). His thirteen books are the heart of Church Age doctrine (of salvation by grace through faith). Thus, Paul's writings should be taken very seriously.

Paul says the following about justification or salvation:

Even the righteousness of God *which is* by faith of Jesus Christ unto all and upon all them that believe: for there is no difference. (Rom. 3:22)

Seeing *it is* one God, which shall justify the circumcision by faith, and uncircumcision through faith. (Rom. 3:30)

But to him that worketh not, but believeth on him that justifieth the ungodly, his faith is counted for righteousness. (Rom 4:5)

For after that in the wisdom of God the world by wisdom knew not God, it pleased God by the foolishness of preaching to save them that believe. (1 Cor 1:21)

Knowing that a man is not justified by the works of the law, but by the faith of Jesus Christ, even we have believed in Jesus Christ, that we might be justified by the faith of Christ, and not by the works of the law: for by the works of the law shall no flesh be justified. (Gal 2:16)

Wherefore the law was our schoolmaster *to bring us* unto Christ, that we might be justified by faith. (Gal 3:24)

This *is* a faithful saying, and worthy of all acceptation, that Christ Jesus came into the world to save sinners; of whom I am chief. Howbeit for this cause I obtained

mercy, that in me first Jesus Christ might show forth all longsuffering, for a pattern to them which should hereafter believe on him to life everlasting. (1 Tim. 1:15,16)

And that from a child thou hast known the holy scriptures, which are able to make thee wise unto salvation through faith which is in Christ Jesus. (2 Tim 3:15)

In none of his epistles does the Apostle Paul ever tell anyone to utter "A Sinner's Prayer" to be saved. Instead he tells them that their salvation is based upon *believing*. More specifically, their faith must be in Christ's shed blood—his finished work on Calvary.

SALVATION ONLY THROUGH BLOOD

Hebrews 9:22 says, "**And almost all things are by the law purged with blood; and without shedding of blood is no remission**." In the Bible, salvation has always been by *blood sacrifice.* God has always demanded blood for sin.

When Adam and Eve sinned, God killed a lamb to cover them with it's skin. When Cain and Abel offered sacrifice to God, Abel's blood sacrifice of a lamb was accepted while Cain's offering of fruits and vegetables (what he toiled in making) was rejected.

Under the law, God demanded animal sacrifice for sins. When a man sinned, he had to offer up a lamb. He had to personally cut the throat of that lamb and through a priest offer the blood of his sacrifice upon the altar. He knew that salvation was by *the blood* of that *sacrificial lamb* to give him "remission of sin."

This is clearly seen in Leviticus chapter three verses six through eight:

And if his offering for a sacrifice of peace offering unto the LORD *be* **of the flock; male or female, he shall offer it without blemish. If he offer a lamb for his offering, then shall he offer it before the LORD. And <u>he shall lay his hand upon the head of his offering, and kill it before the tabernacle of the congregation: and Aaron's sons shall sprinkle the blood thereof round about upon the altar.</u>**

Here, we are told that under the law, a person offering a lamb had to put his hand upon it (signifying it was his sacrifice for his sins) and then kill it. When he did so, he watched the priest catch its blood and then sprinkle it upon the altar. He then knew his sins were remitted. It was all because of the blood offered up to God!

In the New Testament, Jesus Christ is "**...the Lamb of God, which taketh away the sin of the world.**" (John 1:29)

23

He died, shedding his blood, and when he arose, he sprinkled his blood upon the altar in heaven. He has done it all!

In the New Testament we no longer have to bring a lamb to God for sin offering, it's already provided in Christ Jesus. We do not have to kill it, as our Lamb—Jesus—has already died. Nor do we need a priest to offer up the blood, for our High Priest (Christ Jesus) has already done this himself. All a person must do to be saved in this day and age, is simply *trust in Christ Jesus and his precious shed blood atonement on Calvary!*

Now let's back up a bit and go back to the Old Testament parallel of slaying the sacrifice. Where do we find any "Sinner's Prayer?" No one ever went up to that Old Testament man who's about to kill the lamb for his sins and said, "Hey, *you'd better say a prayer for forgiveness to that lamb!*" or "*You need to ask that lamb to come into your heart!*"

That would be utterly ridiculous! No, he didn't *pray, repeat,* or *ask* that lamb for anything. He simply obeyed and trusted in that dying lamb's blood to remit his sins. In fact, he never even talked to the Lamb. He simply trusted the shed blood to grant him forgiveness of sins.

According to Romans 3:25, salvation in the New Testament is by faith in the precious shed blood of Jesus Christ. You might be thinking, *"But I thought you said it's through faith in the Gospel!"* This is so. However, the Gospel cannot be preached without preaching the Blood!

Notice how the blood is found throughout the entire Gospel:

Jesus died (he shed his blood), **was buried** (in the same ground that soaked up his blood), **rose again** (taking his blood to the mercy seat in heaven and offering it up to God there), **according to the Scriptures** (the entire Old Testament foreshadows salvation by faith in the blood sacrifice of Jesus Christ through !)

Thus, no one in the Old Testament under the law repeated a prayer of salvation, or asked God to save them. They simply trusted in the blood sacrifice of a lamb, as God commanded them, to be forgiven.

So, why would anyone think it would be any different in the New Testament? If someone says that salvation is by simply, "Reciting a prayer," they are going against God's plan of salvation, and *are guilty of making salvation depend upon what someone DOES rather than what Jesus DID for them*. They bypass the blood! Eternal life does not and cannot come by what we do or say. It's comes by faith in the blood of the Lamb – Jesus Christ!

Paul shows this clearly in the book of Romans with the following verses:

Being justified freely by his GRACE through the redemption that is in Christ Jesus. (Romans 3:24)

Therefore being justified by FAITH, we have peace with God through our Lord Jesus Christ. (Romans 5:1)

Much more then, being now justified by his BLOOD, we shall be saved from wrath through him. (Romans 5:9)

Justification or salvation then, according to the Bible is by "*GRACE* Through *FAITH* in the precious shed *BLOOD* of Jesus Christ!" It's not by uttering a prayer, or asking God to save you. It's by taking God at his word and trusting in his precious shed blood alone, as it says in Romans 3:25:

Whom God hath set forth *to be* a propitiation through faith in his blood, to declare his righteousness for the remission of sins that are past, through the forbearance of God;

This verse states that Jesus Christ was set forth as a "propitiation" (See also 1 John 2:2). This word literally means *"the act of appeasing wrath."* In other words, when one trusts the blood of Jesus to save his soul, God's wrath is appeased, and he is judicially saved. For this is the only way to appease God's wrath! Simply asking God through a verbal petition to save you does not mean he will. In fact, praying and asking God to save you is to beg him to do something apart from his blood sacrifice already made on Calvary! To beg God to save you vocally, then, is to ask God to die all over again on the cross!

Biblically, salvation does not come from the prayer of a Sinner begging for forgiveness. It cannot. A Sinner can only be saved by trusting in the bloody sacrifice that Jesus has already made.

The famous Preacher Dr. Peter S. Ruckman said it well in his sermon, "Through His Blood:"

"...If you're going to get saved, it's gonna take blood to save you! I get sick and tired of turning the radio on and hearing them say, 'Let Christ come into your life!' [He won't] without blood! They say, 'Share God's love...' [But] they didn't say anything about blood! We have a maculated, lanalized, flannelized, synthesized gospel being preached today that isn't any gospel at all. The Bible says 'in whom we have redemption through his blood.' ... If you are trusting in anything else, God's not going to let you off ... Let Christ come into your life? [You'll] go to hell as sure as you're sitting there. Let Christ come into your heart? Which Christ? Which heart? The Bible says 'in whom we have redemption through his blood!'

...Now there are a thousand ways and a thousand plans of salvation that people talk about getting saved, but the Bible says without shedding of blood, there is no remission. There are two ways to get saved, the Old Fashioned Way and the New Fashioned Way and the New Fashioned Way is

ineffective...it doesn't get them saved. The New Fashioned Way is: Share God's love, let Christ come into your life, let Christ come into your heart, all that modern philosophical positivistic nonsense, [but] *in that book* [the Bible] *it is* [by] *Shed Blood! You've gotta have blood. That's the Old Time Religion!"*

Clearly salvation or redemption is only THROUGH THE BLOOD of Jesus Christ (Eph. 1:7 and Col. 1:14). It cannot be by *asking, pleading, begging, or praying*, for this completely bypasses *faith in the precious blood of Jesus Christ* as the only means of salvation!

In the late 1800's, T.T. Martin (1862-1939) wrote a book entitled, "God's Plan With Men," in which he shows that it's impossible for man to obtain salvation from God by "praying" and "begging" God for salvation. I quote several excerpts:

"When one faces the question of his sins and realizes that he deserves just punishment, one of the first impulses is to pray and beg God to be let off, to be forgiven. Alas! Much of the religious instruction to the sinner is to the same effect. Many feel that God forgives the sinner because he begs to be forgiven instead of because he accepts and relies upon the atoning death of Christ as his Substitute.

But God does not forgive a lost sinner just because he begs for forgiveness. Jesus to Nicodemus gave no such instruction (John 3:14-16). Philip to the eunuch gave no such instruction (Acts 8:29-39). Paul and Silas to the jailer gave no such instruction (Acts 16:30, 31). Peter to the household of Cornelius gave no such instruction (Acts 10:42,43).

The Gospel of John, the one book specially given to lead a sinner to be saved, gives no such instruction (John 20:30,31)."

Mr. Martin shows that man's first desire when found guilty is to *beg* or *ask* to be forgiven. But this is not the Gospel. God never tells anyone to ask him for forgiveness. If salvation were obtained by simply uttering a Sinner's prayer or begging God to be let off, then Jesus would not have had to die on the cross! He could have stayed in heaven and used a prophet to tell us, *"Okay, now I'm going to start a new dispensation. Anyone who just begs me for salvation, I'll accept and give them the new birth!"*

But God did not do this. For this would have made man's salvation dependent upon what he does, not what God did for him.

Salvation cost God something. He had to come down first to the earth and fulfill the law, and then die as a righteous, sinless substitute for us in our place. He then had to rise again and sprinkle His blood on the mercy seat in heaven before He could sit down on the right hand of God.

Now Jesus says, *"All who'll receive me by faith in my finished substitutionary blood atonement will be saved!"*

Notice the oh so important concept that salvation is not dependent upon what a man does (asking, begging, or demanding through prayer), but simply trusting (or relying) upon what Christ Jesus has ALREADY DONE for them. Salvation is not by works, it's by faith alone. And the only thing a man can do that's not a work is *BELIEVE*.

Mr. Martin continues in his book explaining how prayer cannot save us by giving us the illustration of judicial law. He says,

"Every transgression must have a just recompense of reward,' however sorry the sinner may be; however much he may beg to be forgiven, let off; however much the priest or preacher or friends may pray for him to be forgiven....

A man who has violated the state law comes before the judge, confesses his sin and begs the judge to forgive him, to let him off; and he calls men from the audience to come and help him beg.

28

The judge replies, "*If I should yield to these petitions I would be a perjurer; I would trample on law. Every transgression must receive a just recompense of reward.*"

*Would that all could realize that every prayer from sinner, priest or preacher for a sinner to be forgiven, let off, is a prayer to God to become a perjurer. If sinners could realize that, after all their kneeling every night and confessing their sins and praying to be forgiven, to be let off, every sin ever committed is still there and that "**without shedding of blood is no remission**," they would then realize their real need of a Saviour, a Redeemer.*"

No righteous judge in any court of law would let a condemned man go free simply because he "asked to be let go" or "prayed that he give him leave." No! That criminal must first pay his debt to society or find someone else to pay it for him.

In the case of salvation, we are all guilty before God and condemned to eternal damnation. But thank God there's Jesus Christ who has already paid the penalty for us and our sins! The only way to accept his free gift of eternal life and apply God's mercy to us is not by *begging to be let off* or by *asking to be forgiven*, but simply trusting in what God has already done to forgive the Sinner. This can only be received by FAITH in His *substitutionary blood atonement*.

WILL GOD EVEN LISTEN TO
A SINNER'S PRAYER?

As we've seen, many a modern apostate will tell a person that to be saved, all they must do is simply recite "The Sinner's Prayer." But this is not the Gospel, nor is it in the Bible. Judicially, no righteous judge can save anyone simply because they *ask* or *beg*. There must be a *penalty paid* for sins. And, the Bible clearly teaches us that it was Jesus who died to pay our penalty on the cross of Calvary.

Instead of any verses telling a Sinner to say a prayer to be saved, we find many verses in the Bible that say *at times*, God will not regard, listen to, or even answer a "Sinner's prayer." For example:

"There they cry, but none giveth answer, because of the pride of evil men. Surely God will not hear vanity, neither will the Almighty regard it." (Job 35:12,13)

"They cried, but [there was] none to save [them: even] unto the LORD, but he answered them not." (Psalms 18:41)

"If I regard iniquity in my heart, the Lord will not hear [me]:" (Psalms 66:18)

"Then shall they call upon me, but I will not answer; they shall seek me early, but they shall not find me: For that they hated knowledge, and did not choose the fear of the LORD." (Proverbs 1:28,29)

"He that turneth away his ear from hearing the law, even his prayer [shall be] abomination." (Proverbs 28:9)

"And when ye spread forth your hands, I will hide mine eyes from you: yea, when ye make many prayers, I will not hear: your hands are full of blood." (Isaiah 1:15)

"Behold, the LORD'S hand is not shortened, that it cannot save; neither his ear heavy, that it cannot hear: But your iniquities have separated between you and your God, and your sins have hid [his] face from you, that he will not hear." (Isaiah 59:1,2)

"Therefore thus saith the LORD, Behold, I will bring evil upon them, which they shall not be able to escape; and though they shall cry unto me, I will not hearken unto them." (Jeremiah 11:11)

"Therefore will I also deal in fury: mine eye shall not spare, neither will I have pity: and though they cry in mine ears with a loud voice, [yet] will I not hear them." (Ezekiel 8:18)

"Then shall they cry unto the LORD, but he will not hear them: he will even hide his face from them at that time, as they have behaved themselves ill in their doings." (Micah 3:4)

All of these are Old Testament verses, and because of this, many who believe in the Sinner's Prayer will be quick to say that they don't apply to the New Testament.

But in John 9:31 we read, "**Now we know that God heareth not sinners: but if any man be a worshipper of God, and doeth his will, him he heareth.**"

This is a New Testament verse stating that God does not even listen to the prayers of a lost Sinner!

The Bible is clear that God does not listen to certain people, and *God does not save a person just because he prays or begs. God only saves someone when their complete faith is in His finished work at Calvary alone.*

SO, WHAT EXACTLY IS
THE SINNER'S PRAYER?

There is no exact prayer known as "The Sinner's Prayer." Instead there are many different prayers that people invent and call a "Sinner's Prayer," in which they instruct a person to *ask*, *plead*, *beg*, or *demand* God to save them. Some examples of these are:

"Lord, please save me and forgive me of my sins."

"Jesus I'm a sinner, and I ask you to wash me of my sins."

"Lord, please come into my heart and save me."

"Lord God, I'm a sinner, please save me now, Amen."

"God, I ask your son, Jesus Christ, to come into my life and forgive me."

"Lord, please save me, Amen!"

"Lord, please come into my heart and take control of my life."

"Jesus, I want you, now. Please save me. Amen."

"Jesus, please come into my heart right now and take control!"

All of these, as we've seen do not save anyone. And all too often because of people telling lost sinners they *have* to recite the Sinner's Prayer to be saved, many people (and I've personally met a ton of them) think their prayer is essential for salvation. A person like this who *trusts* in their prayer, rather than the blood of Jesus, will then think for the rest of their lives that they are saved *because* they uttered a specific prayer. In short, they trust the prayer *they said* rather than in Jesus Christ and the finished work *He did*.

This is simply atrocious! But this was what happened to me. At age five, I prayed, as I was instructed, the words, *"Lord, please come into my heart and save me! Amen."*

I then thought for the next thirteen years that I was on my way to heaven. I didn't realize that I was still a lost sinner, trusting in what *I did* rather than what *Jesus Christ did for me.* I had bypassed God's judicial means to be saved, and instead trusted in my act of "asking" God to save me.

I further prayed the same prayer every night just to be safe, because I had no assurance. I never knew if I had eternal life, and I was told to just "pray the Prayer" all over again when I doubted my salvation. This I did many times.

It wasn't until I was 18 years old that I heard the Gospel for the first time and realized that salvation was trusting in what *JESUS DID* for me, not what *I HAD DONE.* I then quit trusting in what I did, and by faith trusted only in the precious SHED BLOOD of Jesus, taking God at his word. That was July 29th, 1992, the day I was born again.

After I received Christ, I realized just how dangerous the "Sinner's Prayer" teaching really is when I met a man who used to be a Satanist. He recently had gotten saved, and told me about his years in the occult. He told me that he had contact with demons, and spent time learning from them. I was shocked when he told me that many demons claimed to be named "Jesus." I then remembered the passage in 2 Corinthians 11:4 that spoke of "**another Jesus**" connected with "**another spirit**" in the context. I then asked him timidly, *"According to your experience, how does someone get possessed with a demon?"*

He replied, *"They have to ask for it!"*

I then thought to myself, *"Oh no! If someone omits the Gospel, and then simply tells a person to ASK Jesus into their heart, and that person has never heard, and/or doesn't understand the Gospel, they could be asking a demon to come into them!"* What a horrible thought!

But the truth of the matter is "ask Jesus into your heart" is never found in the Bible one time! Could it be that Satan is behind that anti-biblical, anti-judicial "ask Jesus into your Heart," gospel in order to deceive people and gain entrance into their hearts?

Many would say that this is "far-fetched" and completely crazy. But remember that the Bible warns us in 1 Timothy chapter four and verses one and two that, "**...the Spirit speaketh expressly, that <u>in the latter times some shall depart from the faith, giving heed to seducing spirits, and doctrines of devils</u>; Speaking lies in hypocrisy; having their conscience seared with a hot iron.**"

Also we read in 2 Corinthians chapter eleven verses thirteen through fifteen about: "**...<u>false apostles, deceitful workers, transforming themselves into the apostles of Christ</u>. And no marvel; for Satan himself is transformed into an angel of light. Therefore *it is* no great thing if <u>his ministers also be transformed as ministers of righteousness</u>; whose end shall be according to their works.**"

These verses tell us that Satan has ministers who appear as ministers of righteousness, but are in all reality deceitful workers and false apostles. Could it be that Satan has deceived people with these false apostles into believing that by simply uttering a prayer of forgiveness will give them eternal life? And could he be using the "Sinner's Prayer" to deceive people and gain access to their hearts?

This is a strong possibility, for no where in the Bible are we told to repeat "The Sinner's Prayer," nor are we instructed to *ASK* Jesus to enter into our hearts. Instead, Jesus told us to *TRUST in His finished work* and *shed Blood.*

Asking implies doubt. When you ask a person for something, you automatically give him the right to say "Yes" or "No." Because you asked, he can decide whether he will or won't grant your request.

But when someone promises you something by faith, and you take him up on his promise, he must follow through with what he said he'd do, otherwise he'd be a liar.

When it comes to salvation, God doesn't tell *us to ask him* to save us, but rather *He asks the unsaved sinner* to trust in Him to be saved!

When a repentant soul comes to Him by faith and takes Him at his word, He's saved. For when you take someone at his word, believing him to fulfill his promise, you leave him no other option but to follow through with what he said he'd do. He cannot say no, or he'd be a liar. God most certainly is not a liar! He said if you'd trust his shed blood, He'd save you! He didn't tell you to "ask" Him to do so. He already said He would! Just take Him at His word by faith! Trust the Blood of Jesus Christ as sufficient to save you!

THE ORIGIN OF THE SINNER'S PRAYER

As we've seen, the teaching of *the Sinner's Prayer* is foreign to the Bible doctrine of salvation. It is "another gospel" of which Paul warns against in Galatians 1:8,9.

So where did this idea of simply repeating a formal prayer for salvation begin? No one knows exactly, but it's certain it is only in the last several hundred years that this teaching has gained popularity.

All throughout the early church, the apostles preached salvation by *grace* through *faith*. In the early centuries after the deaths of the Apostles, millions were saved by the preaching of the Gospel, or salvation by *faith in the blood of Jesus Christ*. So ingrained in the mind of believers was the doctrine of salvation by a *blood sacrifice*, that they willingly gave their own bodies to the lions, the sword, and the stake. They shed *their own blood* for their blessed God and Saviour that loved them enough to shed *his own blood* for them (Acts 20:28).

Throughout history, they continued preaching that salvation was by FAITH in a BLOOD atonement, not by RECITING A PRAYER or ASKING God to be saved, and we can still see that today as we look back at history and historical Christian figures from several centuries ago.

Cipriano de Valera, a Spanish preacher said the following in the year 1602: *"Because it is not right to conform the certain with the uncertain, the word of God with the word of men...I again plead to our good merciful God and Father that He give you grace to hear Him and to know His will and that knowing it you will conform to it. And so be saved through the blood of the Lamb without blemish that sacrificed himself on the altar of the cross to forgive our sins before God. Amen.*

Charles H. Spurgeon (1834-1892) said in his sermon Our Suffering Substitute, *"Thou art to be saved by faith in Christ...and in Christ alone. Do not think thou must experience this, or that, before thou comest unto Jesus...Rely not on anything thou canst do, or think, or say, or know; rest alone on Jesus only, and thou art saved. Give up all other trusts, and rely on Jesus alone, alone on Jesus, and thou shalt pass from death unto life.*"

And again in his sermon, The Blood of the Lamb, the Conquering Weapon he states, "*Your hope lies in the blood of the Lamb...The atoning sacrifice, which is your glory, is your salvation. Trust him whom God has set forth to be the propitiation for sin...I pray you accept a present salvation through the blood of the Lamb.*"

T.T. Martin wrote the following in the late 1800's: "*If you are trusting anything other than Jesus Christ and His shed blood, then according to the Bible, you are not saved. If you are trusting Jesus Christ plus something else, then you are not saved. We cannot trust our morality, our good works, our reformation or anything else. We must trust Christ and Him alone.*"

All of these ministers preached salvation by faith in the sacrificial blood atonement of Jesus Christ, not the modern gospel of "*Repeating the Sinner's Prayer,*" or "*Asking God to Save You.*"

So when did this new "Sinner's Prayer" mentality come into existence? As before mentioned, no one can pinpoint exactly, but it's certain that this false plan of salvation is a Laodicean gospel which gained much approval only in the last several hundred years, with its roots appearing to be from the liberal Universalist and Unitarian movements.

I personally place most of the blame for its popularity today on evangelist Billy Graham and his "Campus Crusades." Though he usually preached the Gospel of 1 Corinthians 15:1-4 in his revivals, at his invitation, he did not say, "*Trust the Blood of Jesus to save you,*" but rather "*Make your Commitment to Christ*" or "*Ask Jesus to Save You*" or "*Say the Sinner's Prayer.*"

Some believe the origin of the "Sinner's Prayer" is the back of a popular Gospel tract that Billy Graham loved and used entitled, "The Four Spiritual Laws." At the end of this tract, a person was encouraged to say a "Sinner's Prayer" to be saved.

I quote from this tract written by Bill Bright, and printed by the Campus Crusade for Christ, Inc., copyright 1965:

"YOU CAN RECEIVE CHRIST RIGHT NOW BY FAITH THROUGH PRAYER

God knows your heart and is not so concerned with your words as He is with the attitude of your heart. The following is a suggested prayer:

'Lord Jesus, I need You. Thank you for dying on the cross for my sins. I open the door of my life and receive You as my Saviour and Lord. Thank You for forgiving my sins and giving me eternal life. Take control of the throne of my life. Make me the kind of person You want me to be.'

Does this prayer express the desire of your heart?

If it does, pray this prayer right now, and Christ will come into your life as He promised."

Several things are wrong with this. First, this tract makes FAITH and PRAYING one and the same when it says that Receiving Christ is not by *faith alone*, but by *faith through Prayer*. But the Bible says it's by grace through FAITH IN HIS BLOOD.

It then tells a person that God is not interested or concerned with the words, but instead with the attitude of one's heart. Does that mean that God will save a person simply because he's *sincere* when he prays? No! For sincerity apart from Biblical belief in the Gospel is not salvation.

Many today *sincerely* pray, asking God to save them, or begging him to do so. However, they are not saved just because they are *sincere*. Biblically, God only saves a person when he understands the Gospel, and completely trusts in Christ's Finished Work of Shedding his Blood for the forgiveness of our sins as sufficient to take him to heaven.

Finally, the tract ends in the last paragraph by saying that Christ will come into a person's "life" when they pray this prayer. But this is not in the Bible! No where does the word of God say that Jesus comes into a person's *life*.

Instead, Ephesians 3:17 tells us that Jesus dwells in a person's HEART. And it's not because they prayed a prayer, or asked him to. It's because they have BELIEVED from the heart.

Some would say that I'm "straining at gnats" and "splitting hairs." But this simply is not so. Either you are saved as God says by *complete* TRUST in Christ's finished work at Calvary, or you are saved by simply reciting a prayer.

These are two distinct and very different things. One is a WORK (praying or asking) and the other is not, it's simply taking God up on his free offer of Salvation by trusting in the WORK OF GOD when he died for the sins of mankind. There is a huge difference.

Billy Graham and Bill Bright aren't the only ones who teach this. Many other denominations also preach the "Sinner's Prayer" for salvation, rather than the Biblical means of salvation by faith in the sacrificial blood atonement of Jesus Christ.

The popular Bob Jones University is guilty of this. I've heard them with my own ears in their "Unusual Films," teach that salvation is by "Repeating the Sinner's Prayer." In fact, one of their more popular films tells of a man who is run over by a train. While he's dying, a Christian man tells him, "*Just pray the Sinner's Prayer.*" He did, and then replied, "*Hey, that's a good prayer, Mister!*" He then died with a smile on his face, insinuating that he was *saved by his prayer* rather than by *faith in the Gospel and shed Blood of Jesus Christ.*

Sadly, this anti-biblical plan of salvation by reciting a formal prayer (almost sounds Catholic, doesn't it?) has grown by leaps and bounds. And, there isn't a denomination on earth that hasn't been affected by it's apostate teachings. Today, almost all Christian denominations teach a Sinner must repeat "The Sinner's Prayer" for salvation.

I believe the worst are the "Hyper Soul winning" churches who care more about *"numbers,"* and *bragging on themselves*, than they do about giving a *clear presentation of the Substitutionary Gospel of Christ to lost sinners.*

These self-conceited, number-oriented robots are especially shallow in their evangelism, oftentimes guilty of *"tricking"* unsuspecting sinners into repeating a prayer, so they can brag about writing another name in their Bible. In their desire to exalt themselves and look good in the eyes of the brethren, they have compromised the true Gospel of Christ and turned soul winning into a *vain mechanical sales presentation* of quickly showing a sinner just a few short verses, and then pressing them for a ritualistic prayer.

Instead of telling the lost to *trust in Christ Jesus and what he's done for them*, they usually follow their *"one, two, three, pray after me" method*, in which they implore a sinner to simply *"pray after them"* by *"repeating their words."*

With this *ceremonial prayer* completed, they then write the Sinner's name in their Bible, and go away bragging, priding themselves on being the best of "Soul winners." But as we've seen over and over again, salvation is not by "Repeating the Sinner's Prayer." It is by resting upon God's promise of eternal life through faith in the precious shed Blood of Jesus Christ!

This means that many well-meaning Soul Winners are nothing more than *deceivers* who are guilty of giving people false assurances of Salvation based upon a lie. One must wonder how many people are left *religious* but *lost* by the Sinner's Prayer method.

THOSE WHO TWIST THE SCRIPTURES

Because it takes too much time and effort to preach the real Gospel of 1 Cor. 15:1-4, and because it "offends" people with it's bloody "slaughter house" religion, many who claim to be Christians have shied away from telling a lost sinner about Christ's shedding of blood. Instead they just tell them God will save them if they only repeat "The Prayer." This is a "Bloodless Gospel" that completely omits the sacrificial blood atonement of Jesus Christ. And, as we've seen, this oftentimes leaves a Sinner deceived into thinking his is saved because of his prayer. Sadly, he is not.

Because this wicked practice of omitting the Gospel and pressuring a person to simply recite a mystical prayer is so popular and has been around for so long now, many so-called Christians seek to defend it as Biblical. And, they have sought out many Biblical texts to prove their false teaching.

There are six main Bible passages that they use to claim that the Bible does indeed teach a "Sinner's Prayer" plan of salvation. Let's look at each of these in light of the scriptures:

1. THE REPENTANT SINNER

In Luke 18:11-14, we read:

The Pharisee stood and prayed thus with himself, God, I thank thee, that I am not as other men *are*, extortioners, unjust, adulterers, or even as this publican. I fast twice in the week, I give tithes of all that I possess. And the publican, standing afar off, would not lift up so much as *his* eyes unto heaven, but smote upon his breast, saying, <u>God be merciful to me a sinner</u>. I tell you, this man went down to his house justified *rather* than the other: for every one that exalteth himself shall be abased; and he that humbleth himself shall be exalted.

Some claim that the underlined words, *"God be merciful to me a sinner"* is the Sinner's Prayer in a nutshell, and all a person has to do to be saved is to pray these exact words, and God will save him and give him eternal life. But, this is not true for several reasons.

1. *Jesus Christ had not yet died on the Cross, thus the context is still that of Old Testament, not the New (Heb. 9:16,17).*

2. *The Publican bypassed Jesus when he was so close (Jesus was there watching him) instead of coming to Jesus alone to be saved (Acts 4:12).*

3. *He did not trust Christ by faith. Instead he begged for mercy, which we've already seen does not save a person.*

4. *Whatever justification he received, it was not the Biblical means of salvation after Christ's death which is justification by faith alone in Christ's blood (Romans 3:25 and 5:1).*

This passage of scripture is not a New Testament reference. It is speaking of something that happened before Jesus died. How then, could the Publican have *heard* the Gospel in order to believe it to be saved? He couldn't have.

Anyone who clings to this text as proof for a "Sinner's Prayer" plan of salvation is twisting the scriptures to their own destruction (2 Peter 3:16).

Clearly this is a perversion of the passage and a futile attempt to strengthen the anti-biblical doctrine of the Sinner's Prayer.

2. PETER'S ASKING TO BE SAVED

Matthew 14:28-31 says, **"And Peter answered him and said, Lord, if it be thou, bid me come unto thee on the** water. And he said, Come. And when Peter was come down out of the ship, he walked on the water, to go to Jesus. But when he saw the wind boisterous, he was afraid; and beginning to sink, he cried, saying, <u>Lord, save me</u>. And immediately Jesus stretched forth *his* hand, and caught him, and said unto him, O thou of little faith, wherefore didst thou doubt?"

The underlined words *"Lord, save me,"* have been used by many a believer in the "Sinner's Prayer" to show that salvation is by just vocally *asking* the Lord to save a person. But this is a heresy for the following reasons:

1. *Peter was not asking to be saved spiritually, rather physically from drowning (vs 30).*

2. *Peter cried out to Jesus because he was sinking down, not because he wanted to be saved from Hell!*

3. *Jesus rebuked Peter for a lack of faith in the very next verse!*

How could anyone think that just praying *"Lord, save me"* is the plan of salvation, and how could anyone force this incident into a Sinner being saved from hell?

Again, this is still before Jesus died, and it most certainly is not a prayer of spiritual salvation. We know this because Peter rejected Christ three times after this! Does this mean that someone who's saved can lose their salvation in the Church Age? See the mess one gets into when he twists the Scriptures to teach what he wants, rather than changing his doctrine to match up with the Bible?

Also, in verse thirty one, Jesus rebukes Peter for his lack of *FAITH*! Remember, it's not by ASKING that a person is saved. It's by *faith* (Believing)!

3. CALLING UPON THE LORD

Romans 10:13 states, "**For whosoever shall call upon the name of the Lord shall be saved.**" Many people today use this verse as if it was the Gospel of Jesus Christ in its entirety. In place of the true Gospel, they rather tell people that to be saved they must, "**Call upon the name of the Lord**" *with their mouth* only.

They teach that this "calling" refers to simply "praying" or reciting the Sinner's Prayer and make salvation dependent upon whether or not a person does that with their mouth (thus, making salvation a *WORK* rather than by *FAITH*). This is exactly NOT what the verse is saying, nor is it how a person is saved according to the Bible or the context of Romans chapter ten.

The very next verse, Romans 10:14, says, "**How shall we call on him in whom we've not believed?** Salvation is by *BELIEVING*, or by *FAITH*. Just because someone repeats a prayer with his mouth, doesn't mean he's saved. He must *believe in his heart* at the same time. And, verse fourteen shows that a person can call (i.e. pray) without believing! In other words, a person can say all the prayers he wants, but until he trusts Christ Jesus by faith in his shed blood and finished work, he is not saved.

Some cite verses nine and ten of the same chapter, teaching that a prayer from the mouth is essential for salvation. These verses say, "**That if thou shalt confess with thy mouth the Lord Jesus, and shalt believe in thine heart that God hath raised him from the dead, thou shalt be saved. For with the heart man believeth unto righteousness; and with the mouth confession is made unto salvation.**"

But read these two verses again carefully. They are not teaching that a person must believe *and* say a prayer. Nay, rather they are saying that salvation is from the heart, not the mouth, and that if a person is saved by faith from the heart, then they will confess that they are saved. To confess something is to state that something has happened. Thus, to say that a person is not saved until he confesses with his mouth is to make salvation dependent upon what someone does (his action of SPEAKING) and not by faith alone in what Christ did on the cross. The words, "**Confession is made *UNTO* salvation**," therefore means that *when* a person *is* saved, then he will confess that he his. His confession is added *unto* his salvation (that a person has when he believes).

To prove that a person is saved by faith, and not by what comes out of their mouth, we read in the context the following verses:

For Christ *is* the end of the law for righteousness to every one that believeth. (Rom 10:4)

But the righteousness which is of faith speaketh on this wise, Say not in thine heart, Who shall ascend into heaven? (that is, to bring Christ down *from above:)* (Rom 10:6)

But what saith it? The word is nigh thee, *even* in thy mouth, and in thy heart: that is, the word of faith, which we preach. (Rom 10:8)

But they have not all obeyed the gospel. For Esaias saith, Lord, who hath believed our report? (Rom 10:16)

So then faith *cometh* by hearing, and hearing by the word of God. (Rom 10:17)

Here, verse four says that righteousness is by *believing* in Christ. Verse six tells us that the righteousness of faith SPEAKS, not with the mouth, but in the heart. And, verse eight says that the word of faith starts in *the heart*. In other words, God is looking in a man's heart to see when he is or isn't trusting Him to be saved. When a man's complete faith and trust is in Christ Jesus alone, plus nothing minus nothing,

God saves him, but not until then. This can happen with or without prayer!

Verse sixteen tells us that obeying the Gospel is not dependent on praying, but rather *believing* the report. And verse 17 says that faith cometh by hearing and hearing by the word of God. Thus, the Bible very clearly teaches that a person has to hear the Gospel BEFORE they can be saved. Anyone who preaches that a person can be saved by simply uttering a prayer WITHOUT KNOWING ABOUT THE GOSPEL is propagating a lie! It's impossible to believe on something you don't know or have never heard!

Logically and Biblically, you must hear the Gospel before you can believe it. Also, if you tell a person the Gospel, but then tell them that the only way to receive salvation is by *asking or begging for salvation from the mouth through prayer*, then you are by-passing God's way, by FAITH, and making salvation into the WORK of "Praying a Prayer."

Furthermore, to tell a person he must both: *believe* and *ask God save him* at the same time is to make salvation dependent upon *faith AND* something else. This is a *faith plus works* set up. Salvation is not by *speaking AND believing*. It is by faith alone. Sure one can pray when he gets saved, but he's not saved *by* his prayer. If he's saved, it's by faith only. It's not by *faith AND speaking*.

The Bible speaks about "calling upon the Lord," in other references. In 2 Timothy 2:22, we read, "**Flee also youthful lusts: but follow righteousness, faith, charity, peace, <u>with them that call on the Lord out of a pure heart</u>**."

Here we clearly see that calling comes from one's heart. In other words, calling is BELIEVING from one's heart! And this faith speaks to God (Rom. 10:6).

All these people who use Romans 10:13 in place of the Gospel, telling people that they just have to call on God vocally with their mouths through the "Sinner's Prayer," rather than call on God through faith from the heart, are guilty of twisting the scriptures to teach what they do not. They also forget the cross reference in Psalm 145:18, which says, "**The LORD *is* nigh unto all them that call upon him, <u>to all that call upon him in truth</u>**."

Calling on God must be by faith from one's heart, and this calling must be **in truth**. The truth is that when you completely trust in Christ's death, burial, shed blood, and resurrection, confiding only in this to save you, you are born again. But if you are trusting in the fact that you said something from your mouth, or that you asked God to save you, then you are lost, for this plan of salvation is not "in truth."

To summarize, far too many personal workers only use Romans 10:13 and then tell a person that the word "call" means to just "repeat a prayer." But this, dear reader, can be interpreted by the Sinner as a work that he must do to be saved. It can make a person think that salvation is dependent upon what they do and say. Thus Rom. 10:13, if not fully explained, can be a damnable heresy.

And don't forget the passage in Matthew 7:21-23, which states, "**<u>Not every one that saith unto me, Lord, Lord, shall enter into the kingdom of heaven</u>; but he that doeth the will of my Father which is in heaven. Many will say to me in that day, Lord, Lord, have we not prophesied in thy name? and in thy name have cast out devils? and in thy name done many wonderful works? And then will I profess unto them, I never knew you: depart from me, ye that work iniquity**."

Here are some people who called "Lord, Lord" with their mouths, but God said, "*I never knew you!*" Why? Because they were trusting in their works and what they had done rather than in Jesus Christ by faith in what He has done for them on Calvary.

4. OPENING THE DOOR OF YOUR HEART

Many a soul winner has used this more than once in telling a lost person that they must open their "heart's door" and let Jesus in. They get this from Revelation 3:20:

Behold, I stand at the door, and knock: <u>if any man hear my voice, and open the door, I will come in to him, and will sup with him, and he with me</u>.

But there are several problems with this anti-biblical teaching.

1. *The context is to that of a church, not to an individual in need of salvation.*

2. *No where in the Bible does it say that man is to "open his heart" to Jesus, nor does it tell us that there is a "door" to a man's heart.*

3. *This is not a command to pray to be saved, or to invite Jesus into your heart!*

Simply asking Jesus to come into your heart does not mean he will. In fact the Bible gives no command to do so. Instead it tells us that Christ dwells in a man's heart not by *asking*, but rather by *believing* according to Eph. 3:17, which states, **"That Christ may dwell in your hearts by faith; that ye, being rooted and grounded in love."**

Ephesians 1:13 is clear when it says, **"In whom ye also *trusted*, after that ye heard the word of truth, the gospel of your salvation: in whom also after that ye believed, ye were sealed with that holy Spirit of promise."**

This verse shows that a person is saved when he trusts and he is then sealed with the Holy Spirit as soon as he believes.

Far too many people have twisted Revelation 3:20 completely out of context and compel a Sinner to "open his heart to God" through a prayer of invitation, instead of by utter and complete faith in what Jesus has already done for the Sinner. This is a horrendous heresy, which if believed by the Sinner, will make him think he is saved by something he does, rather than trusting in what Christ did for him.

5. SIMPLY ASK GOD TO SAVE YOU

Jesus' words in Matthew 7:7,8 are, "**Ask, and it shall be given you; seek, and ye shall find; knock, and it shall be opened unto you: For every one that asketh receiveth; and he that seeketh findeth; and to him that knocketh it shall be opened.**"

Many people say these verses apply to salvation, so all a person must do to be saved is simply "Seek" Jesus through prayer and "Ask" him to save them.

Again, we must remember that this is before Jesus died! And even if salvation was by "asking" this would be a WORK that completely bypasses faith in the death, burial, resurrection, and shed blood of our Lord and Saviour Jesus Christ. It is then another plan of salvation apart from grace through faith in the finished work of Christ.

Asking for salvation and *believing* for salvation are two separate and distinct ideas. In the first, a person thinks that by asking God to save him, he has the right to receive eternal life. This is very presumptuous. And in all reality he is trusting in his act of "asking" to obtain something rather than the Biblical means of obtaining salvation by faith.

Some have ventured to say that *praying* or *asking* are not works. However, Ephesians 2:8,9 gives a clear definition of what a work is:

For by grace are ye saved through faith; and that not of yourselves: *it is* the gift of God: Not of works, lest any man should boast.

Biblically, a work is anything that a man does of himself. And it's something he can *boast* about. When it comes to salvation, a person who simply trusts the blood of Jesus by childlike faith is saved. He's not saved just because he "asks" God to save him. He saved based upon whether or not he has "trusted" Jesus to save him, for asking is a work.

Thus, the only thing a person can do that's not a work is to believe on the Lord Jesus Christ.

The context of Matthew chapter seven also shows us clearly that Jesus is not talking to Sinners in the Church Age about the topic of salvation in these verses, but rather to Jews still under the law about "good things." For the next couple of verses say:

9 Or what man is there of you, whom if his son ask bread, will he give him a stone? 10 Or if he ask a fish, will he give him a serpent? 11 If ye then, being evil, know how to give good gifts unto your children, how much more shall your Father which is in heaven give good things to them that ask him?

Notice Jesus says the Father in Heaven will give "good things" to them who *ask*. (In context, those who are his children.) But he doesn't say he'll give "eternal life" to anyone just because he begged for it.

Verses thirteen and fourteen in the same chapter then speak about how *broad* is the way to destruction, and how *narrow* is the way to life. This does apply to salvation. Many people are deceived and don't find the right road. Instead, most twist the Scriptures and teach other means of salvation like "asking" Jesus to save you. This is wrong. God doesn't save anyone simply because he *BEGS!* He only saves those who place their complete and total trust in his finished work on the cross.

"Asking Jesus to save you," then is a modernistic, anti-biblical gospel created by twisting the scriptures.

6. GOD WILL ACCEPT ALL WHO COME TO HIM

Modern apostates justify the Sinner's Prayer teaching by quoting the words of Jesus in John 6:37. They are, "**All that the Father giveth me shall come to me; and <u>him that cometh to me I will in no wise cast out</u>**." They apply the underlined words to salvation, claiming that if someone comes to Jesus in prayer, God will not reject him, but grant any request he might make, including saving his soul, even though he hasn't heard or understood the Gospel.

This is not only silly, but once again a blatant perversion of the scriptures. Again, Jesus has not yet died. Also, the context of the chapter is "believing." In verse 35, Jesus states, "**I am the bread of life: he that cometh to me shall never hunger; and <u>he that believeth on me shall never thirst</u>**."

This defines exactly how a person must come to Christ Jesus to be saved. A Sinner must come by faith or *believing*.

An interesting note is that in the book of John, not once does the apostle use the word "Faith." Every time he speaks of someone obtaining eternal life, he says it's by believing.

A distinction should then be made between believing with the *heart* and believing with the *head*. For just because someone believes in his mind, doesn't mean he's saved.

The word "belief" or "believe" has several meanings. In the book of John, it's in the theological sense of "*Trusting, relying upon, or resting in*." It carries with it the connotation of "*accepting whole heartedly*." In short, it is "*confiding in something from one's heart*."

The other meaning of the word "believe" is that of simply "*knowing*." This is what a person knows in their mind.

To illustrate, I'll quote James 2:19, which reads, "**Thou believest that there is one God; thou doest well: the devils also believe, and tremble**." This verse says that even devils "*believe*" that there's a God. I'm sure they also believe that this God came down to earth in the form of a man and died on the cross for the sins of mankind. But just because they know this or believe it happened, doesn't mean they are saved. It's a belief or knowledge in their mind, not from their heart.

To be saved, a person must believe in their *HEART* (Acts 8:37, Rom. 10:9, 10 etc.) not their *HEAD*. So then there is *heart belief* and *head belief*. How about you, dear reader, have you trusted the blood of Jesus Christ from your heart? Or do you just believe he shed his blood and died for your sins in your head? The difference of salvation and damnation sometimes is only a few inches.

Thus, all of these six attempts to defend the modernistic false plan of salvation, which is reciting the Sinner's Prayer," do not line up with the Holy Scriptures. They are perversions of the truth by wicked men who, either knowingly or unknowingly, are guilty of preaching a carnal plan of salvation by works. For, any attempt to make salvation dependent only upon what a man does (like say the Sinner's Prayer) downgrades the Gospel and tramples under foot the Blood of Jesus. It is then the highest form of blasphemy as it makes Christ's atoning sacrifice of none affect, and thereby incapable of saving anyone.

The Sinner's Prayer mentality, therefore, completely bypasses the blood of Jesus! And it is guilty of making a person think they can get to heaven another way besides through the finished blood atonement of Christ.

The Bible is clear. God will never accept the Sinner or the Sinner's prayer of salvation until that Sinner accepts Jesus' payment for his sins by faith.

Again, Salvation of a man's soul is not based upon what he does. Rather, salvation is what a man accepts when he rejects what he's done as insufficient to save him, and he comes to Christ a repentant sinner trusting only on his shed Blood to wash away his sins.

In this day and age of apostasy, many have jumped on the "Sinner's Prayer" bandwagon. The majority of conservative Christians today are (and have been for years) preaching that all one must do to be saved is simply repeat a formal prayer pronounced from the lips. But this is not correct! This usually makes a person trust in what *he did* instead of what *Christ Jesus did for him* on that old rugged tree! Then, for the rest of his life, he'll think he is saved, and is a Christian, when he's never truly been regenerated. He is left religious, but lost. He is deceived.

If he does go to church, he'll probably practice the same "Sinner's Prayer" plan of salvation, deceiving others while he is deceived himself (2 Tim. 3:13).

The Bible reveals that in the last days, there will be people who are deceived. In 2 Thessalonians chapter two and verses ten through twelve we read:

And with all deceivableness of unrighteousness in them that perish; because <u>they received not the love of the truth, that they might be saved.</u> And <u>for this cause God shall send them strong delusion, that they should believe a lie</u>: That they all might be damned who believed not the truth, but had pleasure in unrighteousness.

Here we find some people who are not only deceived, but God lets them be so because, "**they received not the love of the truth.**" In this booklet, I've done nothing more than try to give you the honest Biblical TRUTH about salvation. Quite simply put, "*Salvation is only through faith in Christ Jesus and what he did, not by trusting in anything you do!*" How about it, dear reader, are you saved? Are you trusting 100% upon the finished work of Christ to save you, or are you trusting in something you did (like pray the Sinner's Prayer)? In what have you placed your faith—the SHED

BLOOD of JESUS CHRIST, or your verbal, out loud prayer you repeated?

If you are one of those like myself who previously believed he was going to heaven because of his *prayer*, why don't you do what I did, and reject all your works, prayers, pleas, and righteousness, and come to Christ alone for salvation, trusting only in his finished sacrificial blood atonement?

You aren't saved by what you REPEATED, you are only saved once you've REPENTED (i.e. turned *from* trusting your own righteousness *to* trusting Christ's blood atonement to save you). Are you saved? If not, why not trust the blood of Jesus Christ as sufficient to save your soul right now?

PERSONAL TESTIMONY

During my years in the ministry, I've come across many people who had "doubts" of their salvation. They usually say the same thing, *"I said a prayer when I was young, but I'm not sure if I'm saved or not."* Most of the time, the Pastor, or a Soul Winner in the church would simply tell them, *"Well, let's pray the Sinner's Prayer again, and then you'll know."* They then show them some scriptures to give them "Assurance." But many times these same people come forward again at the invitation claiming they doubt whether they are saved. And usually the remedy is the same, *"Well, let's just say another prayer."*

As we've seen, salvation isn't by saying a prayer. It's by simple, childlike faith in the Bloody Gospel of Jesus Christ! So, could it be that all these people are lost and on their way to Hell? This can be the only conclusion, *if* they are trusting in their prayer to save them and not the blood of Jesus Christ.

I've preached the Gospel of salvation through faith in the blood of Jesus in many churches, and I've seen many people get saved. Some of them said they had never heard the Gospel before, and that they just "prayed a prayer" when they were young, thinking that saved them. After rejecting what they did and coming to Jesus Christ's blood alone for salvation by faith, they've thanked me for opening their eyes to the truth and helping them to get saved. I wish I could say this was the majority of those I've meet.

Sadly, most people I meet who claim to be Christians have the "Sinner's Prayer" testimony. And when I show them Biblical Salvation according to God's blood and finished work, they become immediately irate, and offensive saying something like, *"Who are you to tell me that I'm not saved?"* Usually all of them then follow this by adding, *"...I know what I DID!"* (Showing they are trusting in what they *did* instead of what Jesus did for them).

I've even had people tell me that I was a heretic and that anyone who preached against the "Sinner's Prayer" was a false prophet. So strong was the opposition against me, that I wanted to quit the ministry on many occasions. This "Sinner's Prayer" Gospel is so strong today and so widely accepted in Christian Circles that most people never question whether it's Biblical or not. And rather than study it out for themselves, they accept it blindly and attack those who try to help them see the truth.

Because of such wide acceptance of the Sinner's Prayer, I thought strongly against writing this booklet. I tried to forget the issue, saying to myself, *"Well, if others want to teach a lie, I'll let them, but I'll tell people the truth by only preaching the Blood for Salvation."* I tried for many years to keep silent, for fear of losing friends, fellowship, financial support, and preaching meetings.

But on June 13th, 2006, something happened. My wife came to me in the middle of the night and woke me up to tell me, *"I just got saved!"* I was shocked. I'd preached to her the truth—that salvation is by faith in the blood of the Lamb—and she said she accepted it. But she kept clinging on to her testimony of salvation of when she said a prayer at age five.

After reading some tracts on this subject, and hearing the testimony of others who saw the light, she spent the entire night thinking and realized she wasn't saved as a child, for she was trusting in the fact that she "asked" God to save her through prayer, rather than only in Christ Jesus, and His finished work.

This surprised me, but I rejoiced with her. But then I thought about how my wife was deceived. She told me when we were married that she was a Christian. And she really thought she was. In short, she had been deceived into thinking that salvation was by praying. She was lost, and tricked into thinking she was saved. In short, she was trusting in man's gospel (i.e. say a prayer) rather than God's Gospel.

This gave me a great burden for so many others who might also be deceived in the very same manner. For this I could not keep quiet. I determined to do all I could to reach others with the Biblical message of Eternal Life through faith in God's shed blood.

Since then, I found out that I wasn't the only one who knew the truth and was trying to tell it to others. I found that Michael D. O'neal had written a great booklet entitled, "The Sinner's Prayer," exposing it as an anti-biblical heresy. (His work can be found at: www.brothermike.com).

I also read the sermon which I've given in the beginning of this book by T.T. Martin (1862-1939), that shows that judicially, saying a prayer or begging or asking for forgiveness most certainly does not let a person off. There must be a "just recompense of reward." Thank God Jesus Christ was my sacrificial blood atonement and the just recompense for my sins!

So now I find I can't keep silent. I want to tell everyone the TRUTH of the Biblical Gospel of Salvation by blood atonement. I don't want anyone to be deceived into thinking they are saved, when they really aren't. Woe unto me if I preach not the Gospel of Christ! Thus, I say with the Apostle Paul, **"For though I preach the gospel, I have nothing to glory of: for necessity is laid upon me; yea, woe is unto me, if I preach not the gospel!"** (1 Cor. 9:16)

I only hope you dear reader will take seriously what is written in this book and dig deep into your heart to see what it is you are trusting in to get to heaven. Don't let pride get the best of you and make you think that you were saved by a prayer you *SAID*. Make sure your compete faith is in the blood God SHED for your sins. Come to Jesus and trust him as your Saviour, if you haven't already!

STORIES OF DECEPTION AND SHALLOW SOULWINNING

Since I've been in the ministry, I've seen so much of this "Sinner's Prayer" heresy, that it makes me sick to my stomach. How can people be so deceived and not see through it? I will now recount some of the worse stories of deception that I've personally witnessed by shallow "soul winners" with their "Repeat a Prayer" mentality. My hope is these stories will encourage you to preach the blood even more, so you won't be guilty of preaching *heresy* and spreading *deception* towards others.

WANTING TO PRAY SO WE WOULD GO AWAY

While on deputation, I visited with a man from a local church, going door to door. At one house, we were greeted by an irritated homeowner who said, *"Oh, it's you guys again! You all come by here all the time, I wish you'd just leave me alone!"*

My partner then asked if he could show the man several Bible verses. The man replied, *"Well, if you do it quickly, because I'm in a hurry!"* My companion did so, but only showed him Rom. 3:23, Rom. 6:23, Rom. 5:8, and Rom. 10:13 quickly. He then ended with, *"Would you like to say a prayer with me to accept Jesus Christ as your Saviour?"* The man replied, *"Well, if it'll get you all to go away, sure!"*

He did, and my partner walked away rejoicing, saying that he won another soul to Jesus Christ!

But who in their right mind can't see that this man wasn't saved? He only repeated the prayer so we would go away! He didn't want to get saved, or hear the truth, and he simply prayed, knowing it was the quickest way to get rid of us pushy salesman! This is not salvation. People don't get saved against their will!

PRAYING TO JESUS OR TO MARY OR BOTH?

In Honduras I went soul winning with a young lad from a local church in the town of Colomoncagua. Visiting house to house, we stumbled upon a sick, elderly lady nigh unto death. He started speaking to her first, so I kept silent and prayed. He then asked to show her some verses from the Bible, and she allowed him to do so.

After reading only three verses, he then told the woman she had to follow him in prayer to be saved. He began, *"Dear Lord Jesus..."* But instead of repeating word for word, she inserted, *"Dear Lord Jesus and Mary..."* He was a bit perturbed by this, but then said, *"No, say only Dear Lord Jesus..."* She did but then added in a low voice, *"and the Blessed Mary..."* He was angry and tried to get her to only say *"Dear Lord Jesus..."* She never would, always praying to Jesus and Mary. Tired of fighting with her, he continued, *"I'm a Sinner and I want you to save me now.* Amen" She prayed that and he rejoiced by telling her she was saved because of her prayer.

As we left her house, I could not keep my mouth shut. I responded, *"Brother, if you think she just got saved, you're CRAZY!* She is trusting in Jesus AND Mary to save her. She's still a lost Catholic. He begged to differ, and bragged to everyone that he won that woman to the Lord that day.

BRAGGING UPON HOW MANY PRAYERS HE GOT

At a Mission's Conference in a "Hylesite" church, I asked the Pastor if we Missionaries could do some visitation for the church. He replied, *"I hadn't thought of that! There are a lot of Missionaries here, and that'd be a great idea!"*

That afternoon, he gave us some maps and told us that whoever won a soul to Jesus Christ would be supported financially by his church.

We drove to the area and began visiting. My partner won two black guys to the Lord after taking them through the scriptures for more than forty minutes. By the time he finished, they were both crying, and made the decision to trust the blood of Jesus Christ to save their souls.

As they drove off, and we prepared to head back to the church for evening service, one of the other Missionaries came up and asked, "*How many people did you win to the Lord today?*" My partner replied humbly, "*I just led two black men to Jesus Christ.*" This missionary then responded, "*Ha! I'm better than you! I just won three people to Jesus Christ! Ha! I'm a better soul winner than you are!*"

Now wait a minute! Are we supposed to win souls to get support from a church? Is that to be our motive? And do we as Christians rate how good we are among ourselves by how many souls we do or don't win? I trow not! This Missionary was a selfish, carnal person who only cared about himself and bragging on what *he* did.

Sadly, I found out later, he told those three he supposedly led to the Lord that they had to repeat a prayer after him, leaving them trusting in what *they* did instead of what Jesus did for them.

PRAYING AND SHAKING HANDS GETS YOU TO HEAVEN

Speaking with a Southern Baptist Pastor, I asked him, "*Sir, how do you believe that a person gets saved?*" He responded, "*It's by shaking the preacher's hand and saying a little prayer!*" I then asked him if he could prove it in the scriptures. He replied, "*I don't have to. Whether it says it or not, that's how we Southern Baptists do things, and have done them for a long time! We don't go against tradition!*"

SOMEONE IS REPEATING THE PRAYER OVER AND OVER

I've been in several Hylesite churches that are very big on "Bus Ministries." I have nothing against these, but am very concerned with their "soulwinning tactics" with the children. On several occasions, I've seen the Bus leader's Bibles, in which they've supposedly won young people to Christ and then wrote their names in the flyleaf.

Once, I remember very distinctly reading the list of names of those that "said the Sinner's Prayer," and there was one name repeated three times!

GETTING PEOPLE TO REPEAT PRAYERS SO YOU CAN COUNT THEIR NUMBERS AND BRAG ABOUT IT

A friend of mine in Michigan went to a huge Fundamentalist Youth Camp as a Counselor to help with the young people. After it was over, he went back home and then read the report in a huge Fundamentalist Newspaper which stated that "400 were saved during the weeklong Meeting!" The only problem was that there were only about 350 young people there!

Angrily, he told me, "*How could anyone lie like that? I bet I know what they did. They had people come down to the altar whether for salvation or for reconciling themselves to Christ, or for prayer. They then had them all repeat a prayer and they counted the hands of those that said it. This they did the whole week! Thus somebody raised their hand more than once!*"

PRAYING SO WE WOULD LEAVE SO HE COULD GET BACK TO WHAT HE WAS DOING BEFORE

With a member from my church in Pensacola, Florida, I went visiting one Thursday door to door. We came across a friendly lost person, and my partner began witnessing to him. However, instead of showing him the Gospel, he just turned to Rom. 10:13 and told the young man that to be saved, he simply had to say a prayer. The person didn't know how to pray, so he told him, "*Just repeat after me.*"

The person did, but then after the prayer said, "*Okay guys, I'll see you later! I have a party to attend here!*" With that, he then pulled out a can of beer and sucked it down. We visited him again many times, and there was no change in his life. And this young man has yet to come to church unto this day.

FINDING THAT VERY FEW REALLY KNOW WHAT THE GOSPEL IS

I've been in over 200 Baptist Churches in my lifetime to preach. In almost every one of them, the first thing I said was, *"We are all commanded by God to preach the Gospel of Jesus Christ. I then want to ask if anyone here knows where that Gospel is in the Bible?"* In over 200 Baptist Churches, only about five of them gave me the right answer—1 Corinthians 15:1-4. How sad that so many churches did not know the Gospel or where to find it in the Bible. And those were all BAPTISTS!

BEING *SAVED* VERSES BEING *SAFE*

I had a girlfriend once who's mother was quite deceitful. She not only was a liar and an adulteress, but she purposefully deceived her young child into thinking he was going to heaven when he was not!

Her four year old heard people in church talking about being "saved." He went home and asked his mother if he too were *"Saved."* She replied, *"Well, your safe! And you'll go to heaven when you die,"* (thinking to herself that he hadn't yet reached the age of accountability, so he was bound for glory). He didn't hear the difference in the pronunciation or understand what she was saying, and then went around telling everyone that he was indeed "saved!"

When I confronted him, asking how he got saved, and why he thought he was going to heaven, he became very angry and turning to his mother for confirmation, asking, *"Mother, am I saved?"* She replied, *"Yes dear, you're SAFE and on you're way to heaven."*

From that day on, that young child has never understood the difference between the two, and thinks that being SAFE and SAVED are one in the same. As far as I know, he's never been born again, thinking that he's already on his way to heaven because of what his mother told him when he was a young child.

Last I heard of him, he had grown up and was in jail.

These are just a few examples of modern day SHALLOW SOULWINNING which is so rampant in our day. Yet, most Christians don't seem to care, just as long as they can BRAG about getting another person to repeat a prayer so they can tell their other brothers and sisters in their church that they've *"won another soul to Jesus."* Modern Christianity is not about bragging upon Jesus and what he's *done* for Sinners on Calvary, rather about Christians bragging upon themselves and what they have *done* for God.

It's sad how few Christians even realize this. Their method of "getting a person to repeat a prayer" is not only anti-biblical, but it is completely ineffective. It produces nothing. It only allows the "soul winner" a temporary means to feel good about himself and pat himself on the back, thinking he did something for Jesus.

One final illustration from my own life should suffice in an attempt to show just how apostate modern Christianity really is, and just how far away they are from God's Biblical plan of salvation through faith in Christ's blood atonement.

THE MUSLIM IMAM AND HIS ATTEMPT AT CONVERSION

Years ago I passed out a gospel tract to a clerk at a gas station, and talked with him for a while. He eventually confessed to me that he was a Muslim, and he invited me to come and visit his Mosque. Not wanting to go by myself, I invited a local Pastor in the area to go with me.

We received a warm reception in the Mosque by the Imam, and were shown around the building. He was cordial and answered all our questions, even claiming that he believed in Moses and Jesus, for Islam teaches him to listen to all prophets.

He then piously told us about how he believed in living peaceable with all religions and that he respected our beliefs as Christians. But then he added that a few days ago some Americans had toured his Mosque just as we did, and that they had "converted" to Islam. I did not ask how, but soon found out what he counted as a "*conversion.*"

As we were leaving the Imam's demeanor changed from cordial to stern, and he asked us to do him a favor. He said, "*I thank you all for coming today, and I only want to ask you one thing: Just say ALLAH IS GOD, and that's all I ask!*"

Knowing history, as well as the Bible, I could not say such a thing, and I told him I would not say it. But the Imam pushed and pushed, repeating, "*Ah, come on, just say ALLAH IS GOD. What will it hurt? Just say it! Come on. Just say ALLAH IS GOD!*"

I would not, and the more I adamantly rejected, the more he pressured me, even getting red in the face and raising his voice.

It soon became very apparent to me, and to the Pastor there with me, that to this Imam a *conversion* to Islam was not by what a man *accepts* and *believes* in his *HEART*, but rather by what he *says* with his *MOUTH*. Again he pressured me to vocally say, "*ALLAH IS GOD!*" That's all he wanted to hear, so he could go away and brag about converting another one to his religion. But I would not say it. I could not, for I didn't believe it. Instead, I said, "*JESUS IS GOD! HE'S MY GOD, and HE DIED FOR MY SINS!*"

This angered the Imam, and he quickly walked off in a huff without even telling us goodbye.

As I thought on this later, I realized just how close his actions were to modern Christianity which too stresses the importance of what's SAID with the MOUTH, instead of what one truly BELIEVES from the HEART.

Just like modern day Fundamentalists and Evangelicals who want to hear someone REPEAT something from their MOUTH, so too this Imam wanted me to *repeat* his mantra, so he could proclaim me a convert to his religion.

Truly, there exists no other *HERESY* than this. For a person is not saved, converted, justified, born again, or counted as a member of any denomination simply by what he SAYS.

But sadly, in our day we find people who are so shallow that they will shamelessly pressure people to say what they want to hear, so they can brag upon how they got another person to "Say the Prayer."

God help us.

The "Sinner's Prayer" is nothing more than man wanting to hear other men say what they want them to say. Like Islam and that Imam, it focuses not on true conversion from the *heart*, rather just getting someone to repeat something with the *mouth*. And it does not produce truly regenerated *Disciples* of Christ, rather modern day *Publicans* and *Pharisees*.

How strange that modern Christianity could have so much in common with Islam, as both only want to pressure a person to REPEAT something with their lips.

Truly the Sinner's Prayer is the prayer of just that—A SINNER. And until that Sinners trusts only in Christ's Jesus as his *PROPITATION,* through heartfelt faith in His blood, his *PRAYER* is worthless, and he'll remain a lost Sinner bound for hell.

MODERN APOSTATE GOSPEL TRACTS

I hope by reading this book the truth of the Gospel is sinking in. I've stated it several times, but I'll say it again, *"Salvation in the Bible is only by faith in the blood of Jesus Christ, not by asking, begging, pleading, or praying for God to save you!"* Sadly, many a Gospel tract does not tell the Sinner this plain, Gospel truth. Instead many tracts simply give a person a "Sinner's Prayer" plan of salvation, leaving the Sinner thinking that if he'll just repeat the prayer given, he'll be saved.

I have literally thousands of different Gospel tracts that I've collected through the years. My wife and I have gone back through them, and been shocked at how horrible most of them are. They might give the Gospel, or plant the seed with a few good Bible verses, but the majority of them get it wrong when they come to the punch line. Instead of, *"Trust Christ Jesus today by faith in his Blood!"* they usually tell a sinner to, "Pray a Sinner's Prayer," which they then suggest thereafter.

Before closing this book, I've decided to copy some of these "Sinner's Prayers" and print them for you here, so you'll see just how widespread and shallow this false gospel really is.

1. THE 20 DOLLAR BILL TRACT

This tract I'm sure you've seen. It's very popular. It is in the shape of a twenty dollar bill folded in half. When you open it up, the first words you see are *"Don't be fooled! There is Something You Can Have More Valuable Than Money!"*

On the back it gives only one Bible verse — Romans 10:13. Then it tells the sinner:

"Here's how you do it [get saved]...Say this simple prayer, out loud, to yourself and to God:

'Lord Jesus, I believe you died on the cross for my sins, and rose again from the grave. Come into my heart, forgive my sins and save my soul. I receive you now Jesus, as my Saviour and Lord of my life. Take over my life, and help me be the kind of person you want me to be. Thank you Jesus for saving my soul. Amen.' "

See anything wrong with this? I do. Notice first of all it tells you that you have to "DO IT" (a work). Then it tells you that it's not just the prayer that saves you, you have to say it "to yourself" and "to God." (So do you have to say it twice?) Then it starts by telling the Sinner to *tell God he believes he died for his sins.* This is good! However, they then command the Sinner to *ask God* to *"come into his heart."*

Does God come in just because someone asks him to? No! There are two conflicting teachings here. One is *"Say this prayer to be saved, and ask Jesus to come into your heart!"* The other is *"believe that Jesus died on the cross for your sins."* Do you see the two conflicting ideas? Wouldn't it be better to simply say something like, *"If you desire to be saved, simply put your trust in the shed blood of Jesus Christ to save you!"*?

For trusting is not a work, but begging to be saved is.

Someone could really be confused with this tract (especially because it never mentions the Gospel one time) and come away thinking he is saved because of his spoken out loud prayer.

2. CHICK TRACTS

I've never liked Chick tracts, personally. But I've passed out a lot of them. They do have some good information in them. However, when they get to the last page they are found wanting.

The following is from the last page of "The Big Spender" by Jack. T. Chick. It states:

"WHAT YOU MUST DO:

Pray to God in your own words:

ADMIT you are a sinner, and that only the Lord Jesus can save you. (Rom. 3:23)
REPENT: be willing to turn away from sin and submit to God (See Luke 13:5)
BELIEVE that the the Lord Jesus Christ died on the cross and shed his blood to pay the price for your sins, and that he arose again (See Romans 10:9)
ASK God to save you. (See Romans 10:13)
ASK Jesus Christ to be the Lord (take control) of your life. (See Romans 12:1-2)"

Look at how it starts by telling a person to what they *MUST DO.* *They must* PRAY. Later, it tells a Sinner to *believe* that Christ died on the cross and shed his blood; which is excellent. But believe how? With the head or the heart? It doesn't say. It, then, instructs a Sinner to ASK God to save him, and ASK God to take control of his life. But is this salvation? As we've seen the Bible it is not. If someone asks, this shows they doubt, or that they think their salvation is based on asking, not by believing only. As we've seen this is a false gospel. When you believe (rely on, rest upon, trust completely in) the blood of Jesus, THEN you are saved. Not when you ask!

3. DAIL THE TRUTH MINISTRY TRACTS

Although this ministry puts out some wonderful tracts full of useful information, they blow it when they get to the invitation. Almost all of their tracts end with:

"Pray this prayer, and mean it with all your heart:

'Lord Jesus, I know that I am a sinner. Unless you save me, I *am lost forever.* Thank you for dying for me at Calvary. I come *to you now, the best way I know how.* I now ask you to save me. *I now receive you as my Saviour and give you control of my life. In Jesus Christ's Name. Amen.'"*

First they say that you have to "mean" this prayer with "all your heart." Does that mean that they believe that if you don't mean it, then it doesn't save you? Does that mean that salvation is not dependent upon the prayer, but rather the "meaning" it or not from one's heart? This makes salvation dependent upon one's *sincerity* rather than sound Gospel truth. For, what if a person really, really means it, but his faith is not in the blood of Jesus, will he get to heaven anyway? Of course not.

Next they say, *"I come to you the best way I know how,"* and then they tell a person to "ask" God to save them. God doesn't save a person just cause they ask. Nor does he save them because they came the best way *they* knew how. What if they didn't know how, Biblically? What if *the best way they knew how* was the *WRONG WAY*? Would God simply save them anyway because they meant the prayer they said with sincerity? I trow not! Salvation is by faith in the blood of Jesus, not just because you sincerely want it and beg for it!

4. THE BIBLICAL HISTORY OF BAPTISM TRACT

This pamphlet, distributed by Local Church Publishing, 902 DeKalb St., Port Orchard, WA 98366, says the following for salvation:

"Jesus gave a parable showing how a sinner should pray. Jesus referred to this sinner as a publican and said, 'And the publican, standing afar off, would not lift up so much as his eyes unto heaven, but smote upon his breast, saying, God be

merciful to me a sinner" (Luke 18:13).' This is often called 'The Sinner's Prayer.' We know God heard this prayer because in the next verse Jesus says, 'I tell you, this man went down to his house justified' (without being baptized).

Will you pray this prayer and receive Christ as your Lord and Savior today?"

As we've seen, this is completely ridiculous. Not only do they twist Luke 18:13 out of context (as it was before Jesus died), but they call *it* the Sinner's Prayer and tell a person that they must pray *this* prayer to be saved. This is the epitome of apostasy!

5. MAX THE COMPUTER TALKS OUTLOUD TRACT

This brief tract from Tract Evangelist Crusade, P.O. Box 998, Apache Junction, Arizona, 85220, might not be well known, but I put it in to show how ridiculous people can get with this prayer thing. Do you realize that people today are just plum "Prayer Crazy?" They think that prayers will get them everything. But as we've seen, salvation is received by Faith, not by reciting a prayer.

This tract, although it is completely wrong in it's plan of salvation, does a good job of illustrating what I've been speaking about in this entire booklet. It says:

"*Just a simple prayer is all that is necessary. Something like; 'Jesus, I know I have sinned, come into my heart and save me from my sins. Walk with me and help me through my lifetime. This I pray in Jesus name, Amen.'*

It's just too easy, isn't it. So simple a child, or even an adult can do it. So please don't delay, do it today."

This tract blatantly states the unbiblical doctrine that a prayer is "necessary" to be saved. It says that one *must* "ask" God to save him. And then it says that it's so easy, that even a "child" can DO IT. This, dear reader, is a work!

6. THE AIRPLANE CRASH SURVIVOR TRACT

This tract, entitled, "I Survived the Crash of Flight 193," by Dale DuBois, P.O. Box 4026, Clearwater, FL, 33758 ends with:

"Finally, many go through the motions of Christianity, but have never invited Jesus into their heart. They miss the mark, just as my plane missed the runway by four short miles. If you want to bridge the gap between God and man, please pray this simple prayer of faith and receive the Lord Jesus Christ as your personal Saviour.

'Dear Lord Jesus, please forgive me of my sin. I ask you to come into my heart and save me. Thank you for dying on the cross for me and saving me. In Jesus name, Amen.'

If you prayed that prayer believing God saved you, write me and tell me..."

Here Mr. DuBois says that people miss the mark (or don't get saved) unless they "*Ask Jesus into their heart.*" He then says they must pray to receive Jesus. In his "Sinner's Prayer" he tells a person not only to ask, but to say "*please.*" Does God save us just because we ask him to politely? No! Unless you trust solely in the blood of Jesus, you are one of those that is "*missing the mark.*"

7. THINGS HAPPEN TRACT

I found this tract in Michigan. It's put out by, "Faith, Prayer and Tract League, Grand Rapids, Michigan, 49504. The title is "Things Happen When You Come to Jesus Christ." The closing of the tract is:

"What love! What mercy! What blessings! What power! What hope! What glory! Do not delay! Come to Jesus now! Pray this prayer:

'Lord Jesus, I believe that You are the Son of God who died for my sins and rose again. I repent of my sins and ask forgiveness. Send Your Spirit into my heart to give me power to fight evil and to lead me into all truth. Help me to love You about all and my neighbor as myself. Make me Your child and care for me now and forever. Amen.'"

Not only is this tract wrong, as we have seen, by telling a person they must pray to be saved, but this tract also seems a little presumptuous and demanding. It tells a person to pray asking for forgiveness (not trusting the blood to obtain it), and then commands God to *"Send his Spirit"* and *"Make the reader a Child of God"* while begging God to take care of the Sinner forever. This is very strange. We do not make demands upon God! We can't beg him to forgive us and then demand he do so and more. This is simply anti-biblical.

8. HOW TO BE SAVED?

The Fellowship Tract League, P.O. Box 164, Lebanon, Ohio, 45036, puts out some very good tracts (we'll look at some of these a little later). But in their tract entitled, "How to be Saved and Know It," they blatantly lie by saying:

"You may pray this simple prayer, meaning with all your heart:

'Dear Lord, I know that I am a sinner, but I am sorry for my sins. I believe that the Lord Jesus died for me and rose again and with all my heart I turn from my sin and receive Him as my Saviour right now. Thank you, Lord for saving me! Amen.

This is God's way of salvation according to His word. Many times men fail to keep their word, but God never fails to keep His Word! Take God at His Word. Don't trust your feelings!'"

What? They dogmatically tell a lost sinner that "*this is God's way of salvation according to his word.*" But, this is simply not the case. No where in the Bible, as we have seen, are we commanded to say a prayer to be saved! It's just not there!

9. ARE YOU LOST?

This tract, "Are you lost?" put out by Bible Believer's Baptist Church Tract Minstry, 5360 East Center Dr. N.E., N. Canton, Ohio 44721, strongly makes a sinner think that salvation is only by a prayer when it declares:

"Why not go to the Lord Jesus Christ and get saved today? All you have to do is pray a prayer like this:

Dear Lord Jesus, I know now that I am a sinner, Lost, and need you to save me from Hell. Please forgive me of my sins and write my name in the Book of Life. Thank you Lord Jesus for saving me. In Jesus' precious name I pray. Amen."

This tract plainly teaches that to be saved all you have to do is say a prayer. Which prayer? They suggest the one they give, but they imply "any prayer" because they wrote "a prayer *like* this." In other words, this tract teaches that a prayer – any prayer – is what saves a man!

Then, instead of teaching salvation by faith in the finished work of Christ, they tell a person to ask God to "please forgive them" (sincerity apart from Biblical truth) and write their name in the Book of Life. But, God won't do it! He can't. That's not the plan of salvation! He'll only save a person who trusts his sacrificial blood atonement to be saved. Otherwise he'd be a perjurer.

Another of their tracts entitled, "Ye Must Be Born Again, There Are No Exceptions!" tells a person that to be saved, they *must* ask. I quote:

"*In your own words, confess to God you are a sinner and ask him to save you.*"

They then give a "Sinner's Prayer" like this:

"*Dear Lord Jesus, I know that I am a sinner, and I don't want to go to hell. PLEASE save my soul and wash me with your precious blood. Thank you for dying for me and saving my soul. Amen.*

If you prayed to God to save your soul, please sign the tract and mail it to us."

There are several grievous errors with this. First, it tells a person that they must ask for salvation. As we've seen, there is no place in the Pauline epistles where anyone is told to do this.

Then it continues by saying one must pray a prayer like the one they list to be saved, and afterwards they claim that anyone who prays this prayer, prays to God to save their soul! In other words, the praying does the saving.

The worse part is the capitalization of the word please (notice it above). I did not do this, I only typed how the tract was written. They are putting emphasis on the fact that because someone said *PLEASE*, then God must save them. This is an outright heresy! God does not save a person or "wash them in his precious blood" because they ask nicely! He only washes a Sinner in his blood (Rev. 1:5) when that person comes to him by trusting his blood atonement for their sins.

10. HEAVEN OR HELL?

I quote from the "Where Will You Go? Heaven or Hell. The Choice is Yours" Gospel tract put out by "Ambassadors for Christ, 112 Sipes St. Winchester, TN, 37398. It says:

"Why don't you pray to the Lord Jesus Christ? Ask him to have mercy on you, and forgive your sins, and save you. He will. 'For whosoever shall call upon the name of the Lord shall be saved.' (Rom. 10:13).

The Lord Jesus also said, 'Him that cometh unto me I will in no wise cast out.' (John 6:37)"

As we have seen, this is a prime example of "twisting the scriptures" and teaching the modern apostate, anti-biblical, beggars' plan of salvation. Here the tract writer tells a person that they can be saved by simply asking God for "mercy," "forgiveness," and "salvation," all apart from faith in the blood of Jesus Christ. His proof texts? Romans 10:13 and John 6:37. As we've seen, this is exactly what modern heretics, who are guilty of preaching another Gospel, do as they pervert the verses and take them out of context to preach the Sinner's Prayer.

I also have another tract from these same people entitled, "Straight From the Bible: What You Should Know." It too makes a person thank that all they have to do is say a prayer to be saved. I quote:

"...Are you willing to surrender to God and make peace with him? If your answer is yes, then pray to God. Ask him to forgive your sins and save your soul, for Jesus Christ's sake."

As we've seen, this is not God's plan of salvation. But the very next paragraph says:

"The only reason God will forgive your sins is because the Lord Jesus Christ offered himself on the cross at Calvary as a substitute for you. Christ shed his blood so you could be forgiven. You must believe this with all your heart."

To the which I say a hearty, Amen! But do you see the two conflicting statements? One tells the sinner to pray and ask for forgiveness. The other says that Christ doesn't forgive anyone by asking, but rather by faith with all their heart. How could they try to tell a person both at the same time? It's either one or the other. It's either by asking, or by believing. It can't be both.

11. REASONING WITH GOD

This tract labeled, "Reasoning with God," written by Dr. Ron Dobbs (no address given), concludes:

"REASON WITH GOD NOW!

Pray this prayer:

'Dear Lord, be merciful to me. I'm a sinner. According to your WORD, my only hope is the blood of your Son. I confess my sin and I ask you to forgive me.

Dear Lord, if you'll accept me right now as your child, I accept you as my Heavenly Father, my Lord and Savior, and my Master.

I want to thank you Lord for not casting me out, but for saving me! Amen.' "

Mr. Dobbs gets so close, yet so far away. He says that according to the word of God, the blood is the only hope of a sinner to be saved. But instead of writing, *"Trust now that blood to save you!"* He instead instructs the sinner to "ask" God to forgive him.

Then he does a very strange thing. He tells the sinner to say to God, *"if you'll accept me right now...I'll accept you..."*

Is this the plan of salvation? Are we supposed to come to God and reason with him for our salvation by saying, *"If you do this, I'll do that?"* No! This is not salvation.

12. BLOTTING OUT WHAT'S?

This next tract titled "Blotting out Blots" by Dr. Isaac Page, distributed by Evangelical Tract Distributors, P.O. Box 146, Edmonton, Alberta, Canada, does a wonderful job of showing the sinner about how God wants to blot out their sins. It even quotes 1 John 1:9 and states that only God's blood can blot out a man's transgressions. Yet he ends his tract with the following words that completely undo all he's just said:

"If you have never come to the Lord, will you not come to Him as you finish reading this, and ask Him to cleanse you from all sin?"

This brings a person almost to the point of salvation (by faith in the blood of Jesus) and then diverts them to another plan of salvation entirely by instructing them rather to ask for the cleansing power of the blood, rather than the Biblical way of receiving this cleansing fount by faith. Is there anyone reading this that can't see this is heresy! It's a complete perversion of the scriptures!

13. THE CHECK

"Here's Your Check" is the title of this small leaflet by Roy M. Reed, printed by Bogard Press, 4605 State Line, Texarkana, Ark.- Tex., 75501.

It gives some good verses and does a great job of showing Christ Jesus as the substitute and instrument of paying man's sin debt. However, the kicker is the following:

"Will you, right now, turn your sin-debt over to Jesus and Let Him pay it for you? There is no charge. It's easy, too. Just ask Him to save you. [Rom. 10:13 is then listed] When you ask, He answers. Then you relax and have that inner peace that passes all understanding."

Here we have a very clear conflict of interest, and by taking what the author says as true, we are left with nothing more than a blatant heresy.

According to Mr. Reed, Jesus will only pay a man's sin debt when he *asks*, for according to the tract, you have to ask Jesus to save you. He then continues, *"It's easy!"* What's easy? To be saved by asking Jesus to save you (a work). But the problem is, as we've seen over and over, is that a person is not saved by asking. For to ask Jesus to save you bypasses Jesus' shed blood and omits what He's already done for you. You must trust what he DID completely!

If you want to be saved by Mr. Reed's tract, you can only get your sin-debt paid when you *ask* Jesus to pay it. But according to the Bible, Jesus already died and paid it on the cross of Calvary.

Further, the strange wording of the tract makes it sound almost as if Mr. Reed is saying that by your asking, you are crucifying Jesus again for this is the only way for him to *pay your sin debt*. This is complete heresy! Jesus only died once (Heb. 10:10,12).

14. GOD BLESS AMERICA

The following tract entitled, "God Bless America," by Clarence Sexton, 2001, Crown Publications, tells us that the way to "receive Christ Jesus" is by Prayer. I quote:

"PRAY AND RECEIVE CHRIST AS YOUR SAVIOUR

Lord, I know that I am a sinner. If I died today I would not go to heaven. Forgive my sin, come into my life and be my Savior. Help me live for You from this day forward.
In Jesus' name."

Right after this, the tract quotes Romans 10:13 (obviously tying to persuade a person that their prayer is what saved them).

Look at this again. This tries to make a person think the only way to "receive" Christ is by a prayer. And it insinuates that a person is saved just because they prayed "in Jesus' name."

Finally is says, "*If I died today I would not go to heaven.*" So does this mean that even if you could be saved by praying this prayer, you still wouldn't go to heaven until the next day?

15. GEORGE FOLEY'S TESTIMONY

One tract I found was that of the testimony of Mr. George Foley. The address on it is handwritten as: P.O. Box 257, Andover, N.H. 03216.

The tract is very old, so I assume it must have been printed well over twenty years ago, as Mr. Foley speaks of being honorably discharged from the army in 1957. In the tract he claims he "committed his life to Christ" (a modernistic buzz word and false plan of salvation) after having, "*...Prayed a prayer of salvation.*"

I will not seek to disprove that Mr. Foley is saved, he quite possibly could be. But in his tract he wrote the following plan of salvation that is completely unscriptural after quoting Romans 10:13:

"*Real simple isn't it? Invite Jesus (verbally) to come into your heart, to forgive you sins, to take over your life, to become Lord of your life. Say it, mean it, so simple.*"

Mr. Foley continues by saying that anyone who does this will have the ,"*...Beautiful promise of sharing eternal life.*"

But this is simply not so. Eternal life comes by "believing" not by inviting "verbally" (saying a prayer).

A person could invite a friend over for dinner, but just because a person is invited, doesn't mean they'll come! An invitation is giving a person the right to accept or decline. And God does not tell us to simply "invite" him into our hearts or life.

He does not dwell in our hearts by "inviting" him in. Ephesians 3:17 says he dwells there by "faith."

16. BIBLE BAPTIST CHURCH TRACT

Bible Baptist Church of Jacksonville, Arkansas gives away a church tract with a very brief plan of salvation. After quoting Romans 10:13, we read:

"CALL UPON HIM NOW BY PRAYER BY PRAYING THIS PRAYER:

'Dear Lord, I confess that I am a guilty sinner and that I need to be saved. I believe that Jesus died on the cross to pay my sin debt. Please forgive me, and come into my heart, and save my soul. '"

Here a person is dogmatically told that to be saved they must pray *"This Prayer."* Does that mean that only this prayer will save a person?

The tract then tells a person to say that they believe *that* Jesus died for them (which sounds like head knowledge instead of heart believe), but that they also must beg for forgiveness (by saying please) and ask God to save their soul. Biblical salvation or blatant apostasy? The Gospel or two conflicting ideas? You decide!

17. THE ROMANS MAP TO HEAVEN

This tract was distributed by the Campus Church, 250 Brent Lane, Pensacola, Florida, 32503. After giving the Romans Road, it commands the sinner to *"Pray and receive Jesus Christ as your Saviour."* The suggested prayer given goes like this:

"Lord, I know that I am a sinner. I want to ask you to forgive me my sin, come into my life, and be my Savior today. Help me to live for You from this day forward. In Jesus' Name, Amen."

Notice that it doesn't say that a person "asks" for forgiveness. Here we are told that a person has to just *want* God to forgive them, and that just because they want to be forgiven, means they will be. This is CRAZY! Do they really believe God would save a person just because they *"want to ask."*

18. HOW TO BE SAVED?

The Fellowship Tract League, P.O. Box 164, Lebanon, Ohio, 45036, puts out some very good tracts (we'll look at some of these a little later). But in their tract entitled, "How to be Saved and Know It," they blatantly lie by saying:

"You may pray this simple prayer, meaning with all your heart:

Dear Lord, I know that I am a sinner, but I am sorry for my sins. I believe that the Lord Jesus died for me and rose again and with all my heart I turn from my sin and receive Him as my Saviour right now. Thank you, Lord for saving me! Amen.

This is God's way of salvation according to His word. Many times men fail to keep their word, but God never fails to keep His Word! Take God at His Word. Don't trust your feelings!"

What? They dogmatically tell a lost sinner that "this is God's way of salvation according to his word." But, this is simply not the case. No where in the Bible, as we have seen, are we commanded to recite a prayer to be saved! It's just not there!

IN SUMMARY

The Sinner's Prayer, or the teaching that a person *must* say a prayer to be saved, has led to the downfall of Christianity and the rise of apostasy in our modern Church Age. God only knows how many souls have been DECEIVED and left LOST by thinking they were saved by reciting a prayer, and ended up trusting in THAT WORK, rather than solely resting in the TOTAL WORK of Jesus Christ in his offering up himself to God for our sins as our bleeding sacrifice of atonement.

If someone makes salvation dependent upon what a person says or doesn't say, then salvation isn't by what Jesus *did* at all. It's by what man *does*.

This is not the Gospel, nay it is contrary to it! It is a *HERESY*. It is a *BLOODLESS OTHER GOSPEL*.

Thus, I am very careful when I give the plan of salvation to someone, whether it's in preaching, personal work, or in written form. The last thing I want to do is trick a person into thinking he is saved by something he did or said! This is why I'm so leery of Gospel tracts that give the *Sinner's Prayer* mentality. I was left deceived by gospel tracts for years, and the last thing I want to do is deceive others.

Sadly, this new-fangled, carnal plan of salvation by speaking only with the lips will not go away. It's been around so long that most can't even tell the difference. It appears to be the same as the true bloody Gospel of Jesus in the eyes of many Christians.

"*Say a prayer*," and "*Ask Jesus Into Your Heart*," have become euphemisms for the Gospel.

When a person says, "*Trust Jesus as your Saviour today*," and then turns around and exclaims, "*Now Ask Him into your heart!*" Most people think that these things means exactly the same thing. The truth is they do not!

Asking and *Trusting*, as we've seen in this booklet, are completely different! One is something you DO, the other is simply believing in what has already been DONE for you.

85

I've been accused of splitting hairs in pointing this out, and many Christians have dismissed this as simply "a play on words." Some have even called this point a "straw dummy."

But dear reader, have you not read enough to realize that the difference between the two is Heaven or Hell?

Because of this flagrant interchanging of terms, people will often find the true Gospel mixed with error. This is why many times within a *Sinner's Prayer* you'll find the words, "*I trust you Jesus as my Saviour*," but then shortly thereafter the anti-scriptural "*Now I ask you to come into my heart and save me.*"

How can both of these possibly go together? They can't! You either TRUST Christ as your Saviour by fully accepting his blood sacrifice to save you, or you reject his blood atonement and instead *beg* him to save you, *HOPING* he'll do so. These are conflicting ideas.

Below I'll briefly show a few more of the many "Sinner's Prayers" found on the back of many other Gospel tracts I've collected over the years. As you read them, note how many of them tell a sinner to pray and ask for salvation while at the same telling God they trust him. You can't do both. For if you trust him, you're already saved, and you wouldn't need to ask!

"Steps to Peace with God," distributed by the "Billy Graham Evangelist Association, P.O. Box 779, Minneapolis, Minnesota, 55440-0779, states:

"We must trust Jesus Christ [correct] *and receive him by personal invitation* [wrong!]. *Through prayer, invite Jesus to come in and control your life through the Holy Spirit."*

The Tract League, Grand Rapids, MI, 49544-1390 put out this small card tract with the title, "Here's a Treat For You!" On the back it says:

"I believed what the Bible said about Jesus, asked him into my heart, and everything in my life has changed...Won't you ask him into your heart too?"

A small credit card shaped piece of paper titled, "Give Christ Charge of Your Life," printed by the Apache Junction Group of Arizona, using only NIV verses (a perversion of the scriptures), commands a person to pray:

"Lord Jesus I am a sinner and want to turn from my sins. Thank you for forgiving my sins. I open the door of my life and invite you to take charge of my life as my Lord as Saviour."

The "Words of Life" printing ministry of P.O. Box 17801, Pensacola, Florida, 32552-7081, prints a small booklet tract of some 24 pages with the same title as their ministry, which suggests a person to pray the following to be saved:

"Dear Father, I know that I am a sinner and need your forgiveness. I believe that Jesus died for my sin. I am willing to turn from sin. I now ask Jesus Christ to come into my heart and life as my personal Savior. I am willing by God's grace, to follow and obey Christ as the Lord of my heart and life."

A small card like tract in the shape of a Social Security card says on the front, "It's great to have Social Security. But greater far to have Spiritual Security!" On the back of this small tract from the Apache Junction Group, they write:

"Now give the Master charge of your life by praying this prayer:

'Thank You Jesus, for dying for me. Please forgive me and save my soul, and by your strength I want to serve you. Amen.'"

With so many apostate Gospel tracts in the world today all telling a sinner they must say a prayer, I even came across a Catholic one that gave a person a prayer to say for their dead loved ones in purgatory. It says:

"O gentlest Heart of Jesus ever present in the Blessed Sacrament, ever consumed with burning love for the poor captive souls in Purgatory have mercy on the soul of Thy departed servant. Be not severe in Thy judgment but let some drops of Thy Precious Blood fall upon the devouring flames, and do Thou O merciful Saviour send Thy angels to conduct Thy departed servant to a place of refreshment, light and peace. Amen."

Now obviously, this is not sound Biblical doctrine. There is no such thing as Purgatory! But look how the idea behind the "Sinner's Prayer" is almost the same as the idea of this tract. Modern apostate preachers cry aloud saying, *"Just pray and God will save you from Hell!"* And this Catholic prayer here says, *"Just say this prayer and God will deliver your poor lost one from the flames of purgatory!"*

This last "Sinner's Prayer" I could not resist putting in. It is both silly and horrible at the same time. And it has to be the longest Sinner's Prayer I've ever seen!

It did not come from a tract, but rather an Internet site (http://777.nventure.com/sinnersprayer.htm). It follows in its entirety exactly the way it was on the webpage from which I copied it, but be forewarned you will either laugh or cry:

"In order to avoid Hell and become a Christian right now all you have to do is get down on your knees and bow your head and close your eyes and pray this prayer:

'Dear God first and foremost I thank you that the events of my sin-coated life up to this point [that] *have led me to this website which You have commanded Your evangelist to post so that I might find the One True TRUTH which is Salvation from my sick sick unrighteousness by being washed in the blood of the Lamb of God, which takes away the sins of the world and I plead with you by the Grace of our Lord Jesus Christ not to send me to the home I so rightfully deserve which of course is the everlasting fiery vat of* **HELL** *but instead to bundle me up in the arms of sweet sweet Jesus so that I may find peace with You Father through faith in the supreme sacrifice of Your Only Begotten Son unlike the masses of sinners who are blazing toward* **HELL** *this very minute because they choose through their lust and homosexuality and abortions to believe a* **lie!!!** *instead of the Truth which your holy evangelist who night and day concerns himself only with the salvation of our precious souls and who will never give up until the last pornography-spewing homosexual pedophile is safe in the arms of Your Only Begotten Son Jesus where he belongs has posted on this web site according to Your Word which is the same Holy Word delivered to the world as that Word given through Abraham and Issac and Jacob and of course all the writers of the 1611 A.D. edition the King James version of the Holy Bible which clearly states that we are all as an unclean thing and all our righteousnesses are as filthy rags and we all do fade as a leaf*

*and our iniquities like the wind have taken us away and there is none that call upon Your name or that stir up themselves to take hold of You for You have hid Your face from us and have consumed us because of our iniquities (Isaiah 64:6,7) and Lord we who believe the truth of this web site and of Your Word know that the rags referred to in the Isaiah passage are commonly believed to be menstrual rags and that is the best we can do as wanton sinners who prowl this earth looking to satisfy our lusts of the flesh like Mother Teresa who is sizzling in the **fiery HELL** right now as she was not a worshipper of Jesus Christ but instead she was a worshipper of the Great Whore of Babylon which is also known by a less sinister name which of course is the Roman Catholic Church (Revelation 17:1-10) but I thank You Lord that I don't have to go to **HELL** like Mother Teresa who clearly knew all along that the most effective way to get her wish which was to swim in the **LAKE OF FIRE** with Satan and to feel the worms eating her flesh along with the rest of the Romanists who of course are busy right now squirming in their vats of lava-grease like strippers in a Sodomite nightclub was to reject Jesus Christ as her personal Lord and Savior by rejecting Your message which is one and the same with the message of this web site which is from You which is clear and the same can be said for all those so-called Christians who reject You in favor of the Romanist system which is based not upon Your Word but upon their fallible "reason" which as any True Christian knows that so-called "reason" is the tool of the Antichrist which he loves to loan to the False Profit to deceive the feeble-minded into taking medication which will only make them stop believing that their thoughts and actions are inspired by the Lord God Jehovah (Isaiah 29:10) and to instead falsely believe in their cause of promoting the homosexual agenda and of promoting the use of pornographic images to incite masturbation and of promoting the killing of innocent babies for the titillation of feminists and satanists who will not be nearly as titillated when Jesus Christ sits at the right hand of God the Father and sees that their names are not written in the Lamb's Book of Life before he boots their smart behinds down into the greased slide that* *empties into **HELL** but to a much hotter **HELL** than the others because they are truly agents of Satan and will sup with him on unrepentant bile in the belly of the beast at the bottom of the lowest lava pit in the **SEVENTH HELL**. Amen.'*

Amen! Now that you are a Christian you will want to know how to live your life for God instead of the devil..."

Boy, and that whole prayer was all one sentence too! How'd you like to repeat that prayer? It'd take you all week! Especially if you had your *"eyes closed"* and your *"head bowed"* as your were instructed to do!

GOOD GOSPEL TRACTS

I'm not against Gospel tracts at all. There are some very good Gospel tracts out there that lay out the true plan of salvation in an orderly and clear manner. Below I'll give a list of some of them, showing the true plan of salvation:

1. WHOSE BLOOD WAS SHED?

"Whose Blood Was Shed," from Blessed Hope Ministries, P.O. Box 73, Rock Springs, GA, 30739-0073 is an excellent Gospel tract. It begins with the confession a dying Christian, Confederate Soldier who says he's saved by trusting in the blood of Jesus. The rest of the tract speaks of the blood of Jesus and concludes with the following words:

"Dear Friend...Christ came into the world to set at liberty the captive and prepare all who will receive HIM, for an Eternal country. HE freely gave HIS life on Calvary to save all who will believe. By Faith, will you trust HIM today as your LORD and SAVIOR?"

2. SEARCH FOR THE ATONING BLOOD

The Fellowship Tract League redeems itself with the tract, "A Search For Atoning Blood." It's written to Jews, but exclaims the Bible truth that salvation is only by faith in the Blood of Jesus Christ. It closes with:

"Reader, have you yet found the Blood of atonement? Are you trusting in God's smitten Lamb?"

3. JUSTIFIED BY HIS BLOOD

One of my most favorite Gospel tracts is put out by the Bible Believer's Tract Ministry of N. Canton, Ohio. It is called, "Justified By His Blood." It shows without a doubt that the Blood of Jesus Christ is the only thing that forgives, justifies, redeems, and saves a sinner. It ends with:

"Dear friend if you are trusting in a religion, a church, your good works, or anything else you may do, you are lost and without hope. Right now, by faith, with a repentant heart, trust the blood of Jesus Christ to save your ungodly soul."

This is excellent! However, it then tells a person to <u>pray</u> the following as well:

"Lord Jesus, I am a sinner on my way to Hell. I now by faith take you as my SAVIOUR, trusting only in your shed blood. Thank you for saving me."

As we've seen, this prayer doesn't save a person, but at least it's not a pseudo-evangelical prayer which tells a person to "Do something to be saved." If a person reads this tract and trusts solely in the Blood of Jesus, he'll be saved, not by his prayer, but by his faith.

4. ALL THIS I DID FOR THEE

This is another Fellowship Tract League tract that's very good. On the front is a drawing of Jesus Christ on the Cross with blood running down his body. Underneath him are the words "All This I Did For Thee." Just the front page alone says it all.

Inside it tells a person that Jesus came, died, and rose again. It then says that a person must repent and TRUST in Christ's finished work to be saved. It even defines trusting as "putting your complete faith in Jesus Christ to save you."

Instead of pressing a person to say a prayer, it asks the following:

"WHAT IS YOUR DECISION?

* I CHOOSE TO TRUST JESUS AS MY SAVIOUR
* I CHOOSE TO REJECT JESUS AND KEEP MY WAY"

5. PAID IN FULL

Another Fellowship Tract League title is "Paid in Full," with a picture of the old rugged cross on the front page. Although it doesn't mention anything about the blood of Jesus, at least it doesn't try to deceive a person into thinking they'll be okay just repeating a prayer. On the last page a person is encouraged to think about the following:

"I CHOOSE TO TRUST JESUS CHRIST AND HIS FINISHED PAYMENT FOR MY SIN DEBT or I CHOOSE TO REJECT THE PAYMENT OF JESUS CHRIST AND TRUST MY [OWN] PAYMENT."

6. SOMEDAY SOON YOU WILL STAND BEFORE GOD!

Pastor Charles McKinney, of Jesus Christ Baptist Church, Highway 57 South, P.O. Box 406, Ocean Springs, MS 39566, wrote a wonderful tract entitled, "Someday Soon You Will Stand Before God."

It's one of the best written tracts I've ever come across. No other can come even close to explaining the Gospel so well. It even mentions the blood time and again, and pleads a person to trust in it to be saved. For example, he asks:

*"My friend, are you ready to repent, to feel deep sorrow and regret for the wicked sins you have committed against the Holy Lord God Almighty? Are you willing **right now,** to repent and accept by faith the shed blood of the Lord Jesus Christ as the one and only payment for your sins?"*

He continues:

"THE DECISION IS YOURS: If you reject the blood of the Lord Jesus as the payment for your sins, you will die and pay the penalty for your our sins in hell fire. However, you could sincerely repent and admit to God that you are a hell-bound sinner, accept the blood of Jesus Christ and be saved from hell

today and forever more! ... Receive Jesus Christ as Lord and Saviour right now, by faith. Call out to Him with a believing heart, understanding that His blood will wash away all your sins."

This is excellent and Biblical! He does a good job of showing that salvation is by faith in Christ's blood, and that receiving Christ is by faith, not a prayer, and that calling upon the Lord is from the heart, not from the mouth!

But with all this, he still recommends that a person humbly pray the following prayer:

"Dear Lord Jesus, I repent of all my sins and ask you to forgive me and save my soul from hell. Lord I accept by faith your blood sacrifice upon the cross as the payment for my sins. Take my sins away and control my life, for I give myself to thee. Thank you Lord for hearing my prayer and saving me eternally from hell, for I pray by faith in the name of Jesus. Amen."

Even though this prayer is in this tract, there is so much truth in it. A person would have to see that the prayer doesn't save them, but their faith in the blood of Jesus does.

7. THE SUBSTITUTE

This piece of Gospel literature from JOY Gospel Distributors, P.O. Box 3347, Des Moines, Iowa 50316, has a bumblebee on the front and in small letters underneath it says "The Substitute."

Though it doesn't contain much scriptures it at least puts across the idea of Jesus Christ as the substitute of the sinner. And in the end it simply stops with John 5:24.

8. CAN WE BE SURE?

I have no idea where I found this tract by Bible Truth Publishers, P.O. Box 649, 59 Industrial Rd. Addison, IL 60101, but I'm glad I did.

On the front is a picture of an aged Queen Victoria under the title of "Can We Be Sure?" The tract is the correspondence between John Townsend, a Gospel Minister, and the Queen. He writes her the following letter:

"To her gracious Majesty, our beloved Queen Victoria, from one of her most humble subjects,

With trembling hands, but heartfilled loved, and because I know that we can be absolutely sure now of our eternal life in the Home that Jesus went to prepare, may I ask your most Gracious Majesty to read the following passages of Scritpure: John 3:16; Rom. 10:9,-10?

These passages prove there is full assurance of salvation by faith in our Lord Jesus Christ for those who believe and accept His finished work."

Queen Victoria replied in the following manner:

"To John Townsend:

Your letter of recent date received and in reply would state that I have carefully and prayerfully read the portions of Scripture referred to. I believe in the finished work of Christ for me, and trust by God's grace to meet you in that Home of which He said, 'I go to prepare a place for you.'

(signed) Victoria Guelph."

The tract then finished by saying:

"Savation by faith in Christ is repeatedly declared in the scriptures to be the present possession not merely future, of those who believe."

Notice that Mr. Townsend did not ask the Queen if she "Said the Sinners prayer." Nor did she respond, *"I said a little prayer once, so I'm okay."* Nay, she said she was trusting in the finished work of Christ to save her!

9. I FOUND IT

This pamphlet, entitled, "I Found It," published by the Bible and Literature Missionary Foundation, 713 Cannon Blvd, Shelbyville, TN 37160, has a big bird on the front pulling a worm out of a hole.

The tract speaks about salvation and among other verses quotes Romans 4:5, John 3:6-7 and John 1:12. At the end of the tract it tells about those who have discovered the truth of salvation, by faith and how they "found salvation." The tract does not concluded with "repeat a prayer." Instead it says:

"You can make this discovery right now...trust God's dear Son, Jesus Christ as your personal Saviour. Then you will be able to say with Abraham and millions of other believers: 'Praise God! I found it! I found salvation–eternal life–as a free gift from God though the Lord Jesus Christ!"

10. PEACE?

This small booklet, put out by Highways and Hedges Tracts, 201 Maple Court, Liberty, SC, 29657, talks about how a person gains peace with God. Although it doesn't mention the blood, and it should, it at least doesn't tell a person they have to say the Sinner's Prayer. Instead it finishes with:

"If you will repent of your sins and by faith receive Him He will save your soul."

11. GOD MADE JESUS TO BE SIN

This Gospel tract with the same name as above was written by Michael Pearl, 1000 Pearl Road, Pleasantville, TN 37033, and distributed at the "Beal Street Blast" by "Banner's Unfurled," 3060 Woodhills Dr., Memphis, TN,

38128. It shows clearly, and in what some might call a shocking manner, how Jesus Christ became sin for us and died in our place. In one place we read:

"The righteousness you receive is not gained by anything you do; it is the gift of what God has already done for you."

It closes with:

"DO YOU BELIEVE THIS GOOD NEWS? He did it all for you, rotten filthy you. If you desire God, and you believe with all your heart, your sins are all forgiven...[salvation] is not religion. It is the person Jesus. Trust him. Love him. Follow him. As you believe this good news your sins are forgiven and God will change your life."

Although it doesn't mention the blood, or more specifically faith in the blood, but only once. It is still a good "seed planting" tract.

12. THE HOLY BIBLE TRACT

This Gospel tract, distributed by Baptist Publications Committee, 712 Main, Little Rock, Arkansas, 72201, is in the shape of a Bible with only the words "Holy Bible" on the front.

Although it doesn't mention the blood of Jesus, it's a good seed tract as it says,

*"Grace is the source of salvation; faith is the channel by which you may receive it (Eph. 2:8). Baptism—or any other work of righteousness; will not save you (Titus 3:5). The Gospel is '...**the power of God unto salvation to every one that believeth**...' (Rom. 1:16)."*

It then states:

99

"God, who was able to create the world out of nothing, is able to keep you in Christ, if you will repent and believe. Trust Him for salvation. You will be safe forever!"

13. THE GOSPEL PERVERTED

This Gospel pamphlet, written by Pastor Ovid Need, Jr, under the full title of "The Other Jesus: The Gospel Perverted," and printed by Linden Baptist Church, P.O. Box 6, Linden, IN, 47955 is as full twenty five pages long.

It tells not only of Mr. Need's salvation, but also tells of how he's seen many other people come to saving knowledge of the truth by realizing they aren't saved by simply "saying a prayer" or "asking Jesus into their heart" but are only saved by the finished work of Jesus Christ. He also places the blame upon Satan for coining and propagating this false gospel of praying or begging God to save you.

His tract is very well written, and it was also one of several tracts that my wife read to help her realize she was lost and needed to be saved by faith in the finished work of Christ alone.

I quote his conclusion:

"Anything less than the clear presentation of the atoning work of Christ is not the Gospel of the Lord Jesus Christ; it is another Jesus...Anything less than trust in what He has done is not Biblical Salvation. Every Bible Scholar in the world can say differently, but that will not change God's Word...It is not possible to be saved unless God's plan is first clearly understood."

I strongly recommend this tract, and usually give it to people who say they "doubt their salvation," as it does a wonderful job of showing that a person is not saved by just "asking" but rather by trusting, for it's the "asking" crowd that usually doubts they are saved.

TESTIMONIES

As we preach the *BLOODSTAINED GOSPEL* of Jesus Christ amidst a day and age of apostasy and apostates who preach a *BLOODLESS GOSPEL* like the Sinner's Prayer, we find that God is still faithful to open people's eyes to the truth. Below are a few illustrations of people's testimonies of salvation who were liberated from the false teaching of salvation by *speaking* rather than by *simply believing.*

THE MAN WHO REPEATED THE PRAYER TIME AND AGAIN

I met a young man who read a Chick tract. He said, "*I prayed the prayer on the back, so I must be saved.*" I invited him to church with me, and he came. He continued coming for several months, but then dropped out. I saw him many times afterwards drunk and following the world. But every once in a while he'd come back to church, claiming he just "Repeated the Sinner's Prayer on the back of the Chick Tract" (that he still had). It wasn't long until he was in the world again. But then he came back a second time, and a third. Each time he said he prayed the prayer in the Chick tract again, thinking it would save him. He had no knowledge, and no understanding, and was trusting in his prayer to save him. Sadly, it didn't.

Years later, I met him, and he told me that he'd finally gotten saved. I questioned him about it, and he told me, "*I realized I was trusting in my prayer to save me and not in what Jesus did for me! Now I know that I'm saved!*" He's been faithful to the Lord ever since!

THE MAN WHO CALLED WITHOUT HEARING THE GOSPEL FIRST

A colored man named Sam Warren, who attends Jesus Christ Baptist Church in Ocean Springs, Mississippi last I knew, told his testimony, and I had the privilege to hear it. He said was a lost man diligently seeking salvation. Not knowing much, he sat down and started reading the Bible. There he read Romans 10:13. He thought for sure that it meant that all one had to do to be saved was just "ask" God to save him. So he ran outside in his underwear, and cried out to God in a loud voice, *"Oh God in heaven, PLEASE save me!"*

It wasn't until twelve years later he heard the Gospel for the first time in his life, and he trusted the blood of Jesus Christ to save his soul!

THE MISSIONARY WHO REALIZED HE WAS LOST

I know of an Independent Baptist man who went to the Mission field as a Missionary. While there, he realized he wasn't saved! So there he accepted the Lord Jesus Christ as His Saviour. I quote from his written testimony:

"I was raised in a Christian, missionary family. We attended every service and visited hundreds of churches around America.

At the age of five, I made a 'profession of faith.' This consisted of asking Jesus to come into my heart. I did not understand that Jesus was my Substitute, and that he paid my sin debt at Calvary...Around the age of eight I was again under conviction. I heard a pastor's wife say that she prayed a certain way and it worked, so I tried the same thing. I said, 'Lord, if I am not saved, save me now.' I did this several times, nothing happened. I went though several more prayers and attempts to 'pray through.' Nothing brought peace to my mind and heart.

I [eventually] surrendered to go as a Missionary to the foreign field. I was ordained and sent out...Incidentally, during my ordination not one of the examining ministers probed my testimony to see if it was scriptural...After arriving on the Mission field I began to study the word of God...In doing so, I began to see what salvation truly was. I began to understand the simplicity of salvation and the finished work of Christ.

Salvation is by faith. Faith is being fully persuaded that something is true. Saving faith is being fully persuaded that God accepts you because of the redemptive work of Christ...as I began to preach these simple truths, people began to be saved. I began to experience strong conviction.

I had prayed many prayers, but I knew I had never rested in the finished work of Christ. I [then] repented of my own attempts to make myself right with God, and rested (trusted) in the Lord Jesus Christ and His finished work as sufficient to take me to heaven."

THE HYSTERICAL LADY WORRIED
ABOUT HER SALVATION

Once I heard of a young lady who went hysterical thinking about her conversion experience. She cried, and hollered, and prayed and prayed, not knowing if she was saved or not. So hysterical was the woman that her husband called the pastor to come and speak with her.

When the Pastor asked, *"What's wrong? What's all this fuss about?"* She responded, *"I'm scared to death! I thought I was saved when I was a little girl, but I can't remember the exact words I prayed! What if I said the wrong thing?"*

This is the fruit of your "You have to pray to be saved mentality." She was scared to death that she didn't pray right, thinking if she said the wrong thing, then she wasn't saved. Someone should have told the poor lady the about the sacrificial lamb of God that died for her sins in her place as her substitute and that salvation is by faith in Him and his precious shed Blood!

MY OWN TESTIMONY OF SALVATION

I was born on July 13th, 1974. I was born again on July 29th, 1992. I am one of few people that have two birthdays in the same month—both my physical and my spiritual one!

When I was a young boy of five years, I remember sitting at the kitchen counter on a bar stool eating my morning cereal before going to school. While I was eating, the thought suddenly struck me that I was going to die one day. I didn't understand death, nor did I know what was thereafter, and the most horrid thought that haunted me was *"I'm going to cease to exist in this world!"* Pondering this thought, I began to cry.

My mother came over and asked what was wrong. I replied, *"I'm going to die someday! I'm going to cease to exist!"* She then told me that I needed to pray a prayer asking Jesus to come into my heart. This I did, and I don't remember much else.

As I grew older, I began to ask questions about salvation, but my mother continually told me that I was already saved, cause I asked Jesus into my heart. I always had my doubts though, and wondered if it was so. I confessed to others that I was a Christian, but I always wondered. But on my profession of faith, I remember my father baptized me in the bay out in front of our house. I thought surely God will accept me now because I was baptized!

Around the age of fourteen, I discovered Chick Tracts, and I followed the formula at the end, "Praying the prayer," as I was told, "Asking Jesus to save me." I never had assurance, and I must have prayed that prayer a hundred times, each time hoping that I'd be saved because I did so.

At age eighteen, my Mom divorced my Dad in 1988 and moved me from my home in Milton, Florida to the little Podunk town of Cushing, Oklahoma. There I began attending an Assembly of God church. I never heard the Gospel one time while I was there. All they told me was,

"You have to speak in tongues in order to have the gift of the Holy Ghost!" I thought to myself, *"Is it possible that I can be a Christian, but still not have the Holy Spirit within me?"* So, I tried to speak in tongues. And I did so at a Youth Meeting in Turner Falls, Oklahoma one summer.

A group of us teenagers stood in a big circle holding hands and began to pray. I remember our Youth Pastor asking, *"Who wants to gift of the Holy Ghost with the evidence of speaking in tongues?"* I quickly responded, *"I do, I do!"* They all then came in around me and put their hands on me. I prayed and prayed but nothing happened. They finally had to coach me by saying, *"Say Hasta la Shund Eye!"* I repeated it over and over, and eventually began to say a whole lot of gibberish. They thought I got it, so I said a whole lot more nonsense, and they claimed I had the gift.

For two years after that, I would stand up in church and "speak in tongues," thinking that this is what gave me the Holy Spirit. Yet, I also thought that I had to be careful not to lose it by my good works.

As I continued in this false religion, I saw things that were troubling to me. The preacher claimed to have the gift of healing, but the same woman came down the aisle every Sunday with Cancer wanting to be healed. They prayed for her, and anointed her with oil, proclaiming in Jesus' name that she was healed. She'd then go to the doctor the next day, and come back the next Sunday asking for them to do it all over again, cause it didn't work.

After so many times, the Pastor finally told her it was her fault for not having enough faith. How sad!

I also noticed that the Youth Group guys and girls I hung out with weren't very righteous people. They'd come to church on Sunday and cry and speak in tongues and get "slain in the spirit," but Friday and Saturday night they were out drinking and fornicating. How could they do these things and still have the gift of the Holy Ghost with the evidence of speaking in tongues?"

As time went by, I missed my father. My mother got a restraining order against him and a court order that said I couldn't see my father until I was eighteen years old. She had told the judge that he belonged to a "cult" because he went to an Independent Bible Believing Church (Dr. Ruckman's).

I missed my father so much, I began calling him and writing to him. He would write back, but usually with a long list of Bible verses. I would read them, but then I'd forget about them.

Five months before High School graduation, I had a nervous breakdown. I'd became very fed up with life and the red dirt of Oklahoma. I was a surfer and I couldn't take not being around the ocean any more. I decided I'd drop out of High School and just drive back to Florida and go surfing. I'd already grown out my hair out long like a girl, and I decided that surfing was the life for me.

I also couldn't stand being away from my father. I wanted so badly to see him again. So one day I left school crying, telling the Principal that I *just can't take it anymore!* I went home and packed up all my stuff and was ready to go when the phone rang. It was the Principal. He said, *"Don't do this. You only have five more months, and then you can do whatever you want with your life. But don't throw away your future by dropping out! Just endure five more months!"* He talked some sense into me, and I drove back to school.

The next five months were a literal hell on earth. I had grown cold and callous towards my friends and family. I despised Oklahoma and everything about it and all I could think about was going back home. I even kept a daily calendar on my desk with the title, "Countdown to Florida." Every day I'd write down how many more days until I could go back to Paradise. I still remember the day I left. It was July 22nd, 1992, only two weeks after graduation.

After a quick garage sale, selling most of what I had, quitting my job at the local Jewelry Store and breaking up with my girlfriend, I was on my way back to Florida, free as the wind, and happy to be going back to the greatest state on earth—the Sunshine State. (Little did I know that only a week later, the Son would shine on me).

Back home in Florida, I moved in with my Dad, who was very glad to see me. I missed him so much, and I elated with joy to see him. It had been over four years since we'd last laid eyes on each other.

As soon as possible, I bought a surf board and paddled out to the surf. There in Navarre Beach, Florida I met Steve Lewis, and Mike Lawarence, two of my old friends from before I'd moved. They too were surfing and we became great friends.

On July 29th, my Dad asked to speak with me one Wednesday morning. I sat down on the kitchen counter and he went and got his Bible. My first instinct was to run, for my mother had taught me that he was a "heretic." But out of respect I listened to what he had to say. His first words were, *"Son, are you saved?"*

I replied, *"Of course Dad, cause I asked Jesus into my heart when I was five years old!"* My Dad then asked me if I could find this in the Bible. I couldn't. He then showed me many verses that prove that a person is not saved by asking, but rather believing.

When he finished, he asked me again, *"Now son, are you saved?"* I said, *"You bet I am, cause I spoke in tongues!"* He then turned to 1 Corinthians chapter fourteen, Acts chapter two, and several other places, showing me that salvation in the church age isn't by receiving the Holy Ghost by speaking in tongues, but rather by receiving the Holy Spirit by faith.

After this, he then asked, *"Now son, are you saved?"* I replied, *"Of course I'm saved, cause I was baptized!"* He then took me to first Corinthians chapter one and several other places proving to me that water baptism is not what saves a person. Afterwards, he asked again, *"Now son, are you saved?"*

By this time, I was starting to get angry. He'd taken away from me what I was trusting in save me. So I thought about it and said, *"Yes, I must be, cause I'm a good person and I do good works!"* This was too easy. My Dad turned immediately to Romans chapter three and then to Ephesians chapter two verses eight and nine. I then saw that I wasn't as good a person as I thought, and that my works couldn't save me!

From there he took me to the Gospel and showed me the suffering, bleeding Saviour who died in my place for my sins. He ended with Romans chapter three and verse twenty five.

He didn't read the whole verse, but stopped at the word "propitiation," asking if I new what it meant. I didn't, but said, *"I'll go get the Dictionary!"*

He told me, *"Don't. I'll explain it to you."* And he did. He said, *"Son, a propitiation is like a substitute. Let's say that you go to McDonald's and you kill five people with a rifle. You'd be a murderer, right?"* I responded, *"Yes."* He continued, *"Well if you did that you'd deserve to go to jail, and after being found guilty you'd deserve to go to the electric chair, wouldn't you?"* I replied again, *"Yes."* Then he asked the following question: *"But what if when they were just about to flip the switch, I came in and said, 'No! Let him go! I'll take his place!' And then they let you go and the last thing you hear as they close the doors behind you is me screaming in your place?"* My eyes fixed upon him, and I answered, *"Wow! I guess I'd be the most thankful person in the world!"* His next sentence blew my mind, *"Son, that's exactly what Jesus Christ did for you on the cross. He paid your penalty. He took your place in the electric chair. He's your substitute for your sins!"*

For the first time in my life, I realized what Jesus Christ had done for me. Up until that time, I thought it was by my works and what I could do to get me to heaven, but it was right then and there that I understood what Jesus had done for me.

My Dad then read the following part of the Romans 3:25, **"Whom God hath set forth *to be* a propitiation through faith in his blood..."** When he read this, it was like a light bulb went off inside me. I remember thinking, *"That's it! That's it! That's what I've been looking for all my life!"* And right then and there I trusted the blood of Jesus Christ to save my never dying soul.

My Dad then asked me again, *"Son, when did you get saved?"* I then responded with a smile on my face, *"Right now! Cause if that's true, and I believe it is, I'm trusting only right now only in the precious shed blood of Jesus Christ to save my soul!"* I didn't even say a prayer! I just believed, took by faith, rested upon and relied in what God said in his Holy word. He said he'd be my substitute (propitiation) by faith in His blood. And that exactly what he became on that day of July 29th, 1992, at a little after ten o'clock in the morning, while I was sitting on the kitchen counter at my Father's house.

Since then I've told my testimony far and wide to many people and in many churches. I can't tell you how many times people have told me, *"Wow! That's got to be the best I've ever heard the Gospel presented."* I'm not bragging on myself, or my orating abilities. I'm just thankful that I have a father here on earth who cared enough about me to tell me the Gospel of the Lord Jesus Christ and show me that salvation is only by faith in God's shed blood! And I'm happy to have a Father in heaven who saved me and washed me from all my sins!

After having accepted Jesus Christ as my Saviour by faith in the blood of Jesus Christ, I've used the "electric chair" illustration time and again, and I've always ended up my Gospel presentation with Romans 3:25. What a blessing it's been to see soul after soul come to Jesus Christ to be saved by faith in the blood of Jesus because of it. As I write here in June of 2006, I believe that about 65 people have come to the saving knowledge of Jesus Christ by my taking them through the scriptures and showing them how to be saved by faith in that precious shed blood.

Now, how about you dear reader? Are you saved? Have you taken Christ as your substitute by faith as well? Are you trusting only in the shed Blood of Jesus Christ to save your soul? Or are you omitting what Jesus did and sitting right now in the electric chair of damnation, hoping because of your *prayer* or your *asking* or your *begging* that God will pardon you before they flip the switch? You'll never make it! He'll never allow himself to be a perjurer of the law. Don't trust in a prayer you said, trust in the blood He shed! For the only way to be let off is by taking the Sinless Substitute, who already took your hot seat and paid your sin debt. Won't you trust him today?

MY WIFE'S TESTIMONY
By Laura Beth Breaker

A few years ago, I read a tract entitled "The Other Jesus," by Ovid Need Jr. It explained how one is not saved by simply praying "*Jesus, please come into my heart and save me.*" I never heard this until that day. I said that prayer when I was five years old. And as "assurance," I prayed it again at age thirteen and a few other times before I read this tract.

The tract explained further that salvation is only by trusting in the finished work and shed blood of Jesus Christ. Despite the truth, I justified my experience of praying when I was five by saying to myself that I believed Jesus died to save me and that God knew what was in my heart. I thought to myself that even if I didn't fully understand the Gospel when I was five, surely I did before I asked God to save me again when I was thirteen.

But nonetheless after I read this tract, I prayed in my heart, "Lord God, *if* I'm not saved, I'm trusting only in the finished work on Calvary right now," (just to cover all my bases). I did this again about a half a dozen times over the next couple of years.

I didn't realize then that my prayers of "assurance" showed I had doubts. But my "ifs" proved I still held onto believing I was saved when I was five.

Then one day I read a tract called, "The Bloodless Gospel." It showed how the ecumenical, apostate crowd preaches that someone is saved by "turning their life over to God," or "making a decision for Christ." But this is not the plan of salvation, even if one heard that Christ died for their sins. I questioned within myself, "Was what I did similar to this teaching?"

The next day another such tract came across my hands. Written in the 1800's it was called, "No Forgiveness Without Blood," by T. T. Martin. I quote the tract:

"When one faces the question of his sins and realizes that he deserves just punishment, one of the first impulses is to pray and beg God to be let off, to be forgiven. Alas! Much of the religious instruction to the sinner is to the same effect. Many feel that God forgives the sinner because he begs to be forgiven instead of because he accepts and relies upon the atoning death of Christ as his Substitute."

When I read this, the truth finally sunk in. This was exactly what I did when I was five years old. I may have had the right Gospel, (i.e. Jesus Christ died to save me) but in my heart I thought that if I believed what He did for me *and* if I only *asked* God to save me, he would, knowing the sincerity of my desire that I *wanted* to be saved. I had the right gospel, but the wrong plan of salvation. Asking and trusting are conflicting ideas. Really it was faith plus works although I didn't recognize it for that at the time.

But, I managed to shrug all that off too as since then I have said within my heart that even IF I was not saved then, I am trusting in his blood now and that's what counts.

The very next day I heard a story of a ten-year-old boy who went to vacation Bible school and prayed and asked Jesus to come into his heart and save him. He was so excited that he went and told his grandfather about it. But after some discussion and studying of the Bible this ten-year-old boy realized he was not saved at all by *asking* God to save him no matter how sincere he was. And so it was right then that he put his faith in nothing less than Jesus' blood and righteousness.

The day after this, I was reading a church newsletter with an article about this very same subject. A preacher (who had asked Jesus into his heart when he was five) went to the mission field. After doing some studying on the subject of salvation he realized he wasn't saved at all and finally put his faith solely in the shed blood of Jesus to save him.

I couldn't sleep that night. I stayed up for hours thinking on these things and how I've tried to justify what I had believed as salvation.

I then realized there was *no way* I could have been saved when I was five, or when I was 13 or any other time when I prayed and asked God to save me. Why then, when I learned the truth of what salvation was, was I still praying, "**IF** I'm not saved..." My "ifs" proved to me that I still held onto the idea that I was saved when I was five, when I wasn't.

It wasn't until this night (June 13th, 2006) that I repented of all my prayers and all my sincerity as salvation. It wasn't until this night that I realized I was lost! Finally there was nothing left for me to rest in for salvation but the FINISHED work of Jesus on the cross - that is, His shed blood. That's when I took God at his word, and received Him by faith. And I didn't even have to manifest that faith with a prayer.

All those other times that I had said a prayer within myself, I never told anyone about it. I thought it was just as well that people kept believing what I already told them about when I supposedly got saved. But this night I couldn't keep it to myself. I had to tell my husband about it. And now I have to tell my friends and family about it too.

Many are deceived like I was. It is as if Jesus is saying, "*Look, I've done the work already needed to save you. There's the blood on the altar. All you have to do is trust in that work. Do you?*" And one responds, "*Jesus, I believe you died on the cross to save me, now will you save me?*" Or, "*I'm trusting that you will save me if I want to be saved - God I want to be saved!*" Or, "*God save me!*" Or, "*Lord God, you gave your life for me, now I give my life to you. Please save me today!*" Or, "*Jesus will you come into my heart and save me?*" Or, "*God please forgive my sins and save me.*" These are all false plans of salvation. And Jesus is left still saying, "*I've DONE the work needed to save you! I've already shed my blood for you. Will you just trust in that cleansing blood?"* Yet still someone asks, *" Jesus, will you save me?"*

Just knowing what the Gospel is isn't salvation. Sincerely admitting to God your damnation without Him and your desire to be saved isn't either. Only faith in the finished work of Jesus on the cross, that is, His shed, cleansing blood, is salvation.

Now tell me if you can find the plan of salvation in these "simple" steps:

1. *Admit you are a sinner.*
2. *Be willing to turn from sin (repent).*
3. *Believe that Jesus Christ died for you.*
4. *Through prayer, invite Jesus into your Life to become your personal Saviour.*

Just knowing that Jesus died for you is not the plan of salvation. You can believe in your mind, not in your heart. Inviting Jesus into your life is not, according to the Bible, the plan God set forth for salvation either. (Christ does dwell in the heart of a believer by faith according to Ephesians 3:17, but not by asking or inviting). God has set forth Jesus to be our salvation *through faith in His blood.* Rom. 3:25 states, "Whom God hath set forth *to be* a propitiation through **faith** in his blood..."

Jesus only becomes our personal Saviour when we accept his finished work by faith. Not when we *ask* him to be our Saviour, and not when we beg him to do so.

Do these simple steps remind you of something that a charismatic preacher might say to get the people to "make a decision?" These 4 simple steps come straight from the last page of nearly every Chick Track. I know of so many people who have followed these steps and confess they are saved, but have doubts so often that they pray step number 4 in their hearts once a year or more for "assurance," or "just to cover all their bases."

And when you ask them their testimony they will say they were saved when they *prayed.* Yet another may say when they believed and *prayed.* But Believing *and* praying is not the plan of salvation. That is faith and works!

After having my eyes opened to that fact, I went through my husband's big box of tracts to see what each one had to say about how to get saved. 99.5% of them said something to this affect:

"If you've never received Jesus Christ as your Saviour, bow your head this minute and ask Jesus to save you."

I couldn't believe it. Could so many "Christians" really be so deceived?

I used to think that almost everyone who was saved had doubts occasionally. But now I can see that a lot of people, who think they are saved by this method, AREN'T. No wonder they have doubts!

I know there may be some people who read this and will say that I was saved the whole time. They will think I'm probably mixed up in some cult religion that tries to talk people out of their salvation. They may be angry at me for writing at all and encouraging suspicion in the minds of others about their own salvation.

But it is for those people who have had doubts that I am writing this. The Bible says for us to examine our hearts. 2 Cor. 13:5 says, "**Examine yourselves, whether ye be in the faith; prove your own selves...**"

I know that I know that I know that I'm saved by grace through faith in the blood of Jesus. How about you?

If you were saved by reading this book, or it was just an encouragement to you and you'd like to tell me about it, please feel free to email me at:

Robertbreaker3@hotmail.com

ABOUT THE AUTHOR

Robert Ray Breaker III is a King James Bible Believing Independent Baptist. His father led him to the Lord on July 29, 1992 in Milton, Florida.

A few years later he enrolled in the Pensacola Bible Institute and graduated there in 1998 with a Bachelors of Divinity.

While attending Bible School, Robert pastored, Garcon Point Baptist Church for a short time.

Two weeks after graduation, Robert went to Honduras, where he eventually became a Missionary for seven years on the field, planting several churches.

Today Robert is a member of an Independent Baptist church in Monterrey, Mexico, and travels extensively throughout Central, South, and even North America fulfilling his God-called ministry as a Missionary Evangelist to the Spanish speaking people.

He also desires to reach his own English Speaking people in this day and age of apostasy, compelling them to return to the old time way, and stand firmly on the Biblical doctrines of **salvation**, **sanctification**, *and* **the holy scriptures**.

Bro. Breaker also runs BREAKER PUBLICATIONS, a small printing ministry, focusing on printing good, sound, biblical literature.

Other Works by the Same author:

*What the Bible Says about Marriage,
Divorce, and Remarriage*

Biblical Study Notes on Various Topics for Bible Believers

Why I am more than Just a Fundamentalist!

A Brief History of the Spanish Bible

The History and Truth about the Spanish Bible Issue

The Heresy of the Sinner's Prayer

Hey, Where's the Blood?

Why I am a Baptist

A Brief History of the Spanish Bible

The Truth About the Spanish Bible Controversy

The Truth about the Modern Gomez Spanish Bible

*The Spanish Bible and Those
Courageous men Behind its Inception*

Brought to you by:

Breaker's

Publications

740 Mike Gibson Lane
Milton, Florida 32583

Email: **Robertbreaker3@hotmail.com**
Website: **www.rrb3.com**

Made in the USA
Lexington, KY
07 February 2015